Hammock:
How To Make Your Own
and Lie in It

Hammock: How to Make Your Own and Lie in It

By Denison Andrews

Workman Publishing Company
New York

Jacket photo by Jerry Darvin
Illustrations by Norma Erler Rahn

All rights reserved.
© *Copyright 1972, 1978 by Denison Andrews*
This book may not be reproduced in whole
or in part, by mimeograph or any other means,
without permission in writing.

First printing March 1978

Workman Publishing Company
1 West 39 Street
New York, New York 10018
Printed in the United States of America.

Library of Congress Cataloging in Publication Data
Andrews, Denison, 1935–
Hammock: How to make your own and lie in it.
  1. Hammocks. I. Title.
TT849.2.A5   1978   746.9   77-28517
ISBN 0-89480-028-0

Acknowledgments

Many people helped me in writing this book. Sandy Cohen, the Hammock Master of New York, gave me information on the Maya Indians and on the problems of installing hammocks. Miss Rina P. Prentice of the Department of Weapons, Equipment and Relics at the National Maritime Museum, Greenwich, England, sent me useful historical data. Celia Eller's knowledge of fabrics and sewing helped me with the naval and Brazilian hammocks. Joanne Segal Brandford introduced me to the sprang hammock. Her student, Angela Kimberk, gave me my first weaving lessons. The members of the Twin Oaks Community contributed both their hospitality and knowledge during one of the most interesting weeks of my life.

My special thanks goes to my psychiatrist, Dr. Leonard Friedman, who, in one visit, convinced me that "writer's block" was not an incurable neurosis.

My deepest gratitude goes to my lover and wife who knows, as only she could know, how to encourage me, how to prod me, and when to let me flounder alone. It is a small token of what I feel and what I owe when I dedicate this little book to Patricia Caplan.

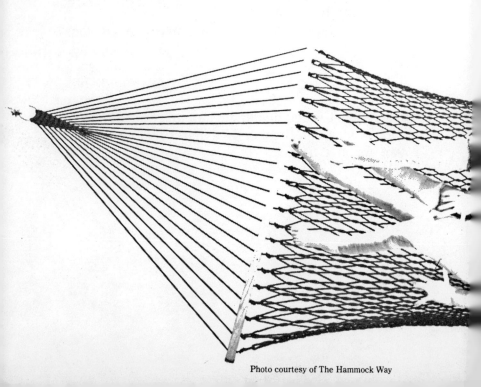

Photo courtesy of The Hammock Way

Contents

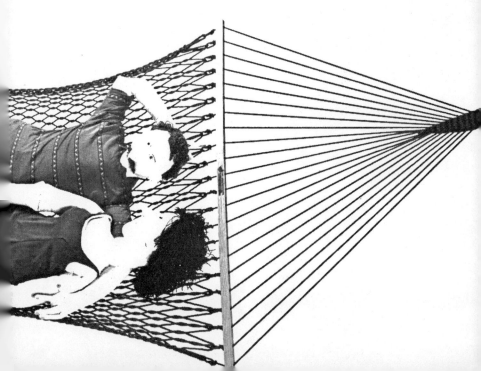

How I Became an Expert

I have always wanted to be an Expert. The image of the Expert — a person who knows the most about something, anything, from steam calliopes to baboons — has always filled me with longing. Expertise: that supreme status, the sheer competence of it! And the more tangible rewards: who would you ask to fix your steam calliope; or your baboon, but the Expert? Consultant fees. *What's My Line?* "What do you do?" people ask at parties. Pity the banker. Pity the systems analyst. I am an Expert — at hammocks.

It all began when someone sent me a clipping about giant Yucatan hammocks. I had been in a hammock a few years before and now wanted to see these Mayan wonders. I was dazzled by their beauty and comfort, so dazzled that I saw them as the answer to the small-apartment problem and opened a hammock store in Cambridge, Mass., an interesting city full of small apartments. Unfortunately, I learned that hammocks are habit-forming and tend to destroy the competitive spirit so necessary for business success. But did I ever have fun on my way to bankruptcy!

It was a beautiful shop, right on Massachusetts Avenue, with three brightly colored hammocks on display and the walls covered with second-rate but charming Balinese art. Some days, it was the best party in town. Anybody interesting was served wine. Occasionally, I would open at midnight and let a dozen characters in to frolic in the hammocks. I slept in the store for a while, in a hammock, but it was too public to be a bedroom and policemen's flashlights make me paranoid at 3:00 A.M. With a friend, I perfected the amazing acrobatic feat of a double-flying-mid-air-hammock-exchange. When business was slow, I relaxed in a hammock. *What better way to make a living?* thought I, even though I wasn't. Once a customer had to wake me up for service and, on a few occasions, I let customers sleep until closing, a good rest for them and a good advertisement for my shop.

Owning a hammock store meant I talked a lot about hammocks. People told me about their hammocks or brought them in for my inspection. Friends and relatives sent me clippings, mostly "Big George" cartoons by Virgil Partch. I looked for hammocks when I visited museums. A local daytime television personality invited me to appear on his show, the topic being Sleep. I heard myself introduced as a "hammock historian." *Wow!* thought I, *That sounds pretty good!* This was my first heady taste of being an Expert. I started doing some research in history and ethnography and discovered the secret of The Easy Way to Become an Expert which I will pass on to you: pick an area where no one knows anything at all and learn a little bit about it. The trouble with a noncompetitive field, however, is that there is no Nobel Prize awarded in it. But if you can't be a genius, you might as well become an Expert.

All this led me to figure out how to make hammocks. Now that you know the author is not an old salt who sits on coils of rope, amazing children by tying intricate knots, or whittling hammock spreaders with the knife he carries in his boot, let me go on to assure you I am also not a clever sort with a house full of wonderful things I have made out of objects found in garbage cans, nor am I a skilled craftsman with a studio filled with tools and looms. I am Everyman, with five thumbs firmly planted on each hand. If I could figure out how to make all these hammocks without this little book of instructions, then you can certainly figure out how to make a hammock *with* this book of instructions.

I try not to sound like the Omniscient Instructor, because Omniscient Instructors in "how-to" books notoriously fade away when you need them the most — perhaps to maintain their omniscience. The Expert, in this case, is merely someone who went through it all first. To a skilled craftsperson, these instructions may seem belabored. I would rather err on this side than on the side of obscurity because I really hope to spare the reader some of the messes I got myself into. At times, I have to ask you to follow my instructions on blind faith, as in assembling a radio kit, but I try to predict the next island of confidence, and to give you some idea of the tolerable margin of error. Hammock-making is not a precise skill. You probably will occasionally come up with a better technique than mine.

The final advantage of becoming an Expert is you get to write a book about it. Here it is.

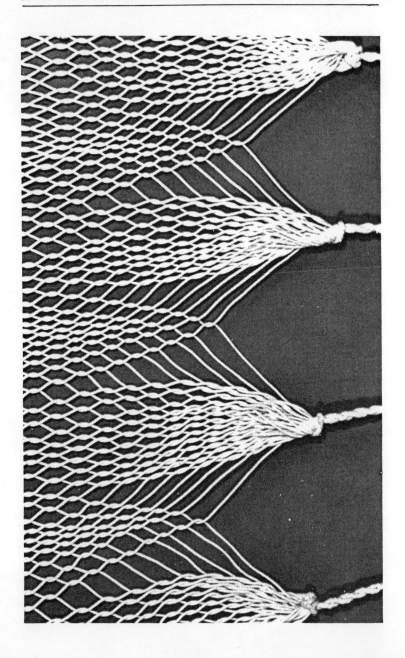

Hammock History

Hammock'(hæ·mek). **Forms:** *a.* **6–9 hamaca, 7 acca, -acco, -ackoe, hammacho, 8 hamacoe, 8–9 hammacoe.** *β.* **7 hamack(e, hammac(k, -aque, amack, hamock, hammok, 8 hammoc, 8–9 hamac, 7- hammock. [4. Sp.** *hamaca* **of Carib origin; cf. F.** *hamac* **(1555 in Hatz.-Darm.).]**
1. A hanging bed, consisting of a large piece of canvas, netting, etc. suspended by cords at both ends; used esp. by sailors on board ship, also in hot climates or seasons on land.
a **1555** Eden *Decades* 200 Theyr hangynge beddes whiche they caule *Hamacas.* **1596** Raleigh *Discov. Gviana* 55. They lay each of them in a cotten Hamaca, which we call brasill beds. **1613** R. Harcourt *Voy. Guiana In Harl, Misc.* (Malh) III 191 Hamaccas, which are Indian beds, most necessary in those parts. **1638** Sir T. Herbert *Trav.* (ed. 2) 7 Saylers, who . . get forthwith into their beds (or hamackoes) [**1677** or hamacks]. **1761** *London Mag.* XXX. 220 Orders were . . given for sewing him up in a hamacoe, in order to bury him. **1794** *Rigging & Seamanship* I. 170 To keep the hamacoes in the stantions. **1847** Prescott *Peru* (1850) II, 101 Carried on the shoulders of the natives in the *hamacas,* or sedans, of the country.
β **1626** Capt. Smith *Accid. Yng. Seamen* 11 A Hamacke, the lockers, the round-house. **1657** R. Ligon *Barbadoes* (1673) 45 Lye down and rest them in their Hamocks. **1675** *Mistaken Husband* v i. in *Dryden's Wks.* (1884) VIII. 626 It cannot be so convenient as a Hammaque. **1698** Froger *Voy.* 134 There is nothing but Famine that can draw them out of their Amacks. **1723** J. Atkins *Voy. Guinea* (1735) 112 Travelling is in Hammocks . . slung cross a Pole and bore up at each end by a Negro. **1804** Nelson 26 Apr. in Nicolas *Disp.* (1845) V. 514 Seamen's beds and hammocks are very much wanted. **1840** R H. Dana *Bef. Mast* xxviii. 93, I went aboard, and turned into my hammock.

T his delightful entry in *The Oxford English Dictionary* indicates how long it took the English language to figure out how to spell the word. The origin of hammocks themselves goes back to pre-Columbian antiquity, somewhere between southern Brazil and central Mexico. Perhaps some-one took a nap in a fishnet that had been hung up to dry and the idea caught on. Hammocks make a lot of sense in a hot climate.

A week after his miscalculations had brought Columbus to the New World, he saw "hamacs" of cotton on the island of Exuma, near San Salvador in the Bahamas.* The 1698 entry from Froger's *Voyages:* "There is nothing but Famine that can draw them out of their Amacks," may go part way toward explaining the ease of the Spanish and Portuguese conquests. Or, perhaps, after the Indians had been worked over by these greedy types, they needed the rest. Hammocks do not seem to have had any parallel development elsewhere in the world. The Portuguese spread them around, especially to Africa where they caught on not so much as beds but as a means of transportation. Great White Bwana fancied being carried around in a hammock, slung from a pole, by a team of native bearers. Some people will do anything to avoid work. This manner of travel was quickly copied by the local gentry in Africa.

Outside of their land of origin, the use of hammocks was almost entirely limited to the navies of Europe. One naval chauvinist, Admiral W. H. Smythe in his *Sailor's Word Book,* goes so far as to claim them in all but name: "Hammock: A swinging sea-bed, the undisputed invention of Alcibiades; but the modern name is derived from the carribs. . . ." The first authorized British Navy payment for hammock canvas was made in 1597 ". . . for the better

*Washington Irving, *History of the Life and Voyages of Columbus,* Book IV Chapter 2, New York, 1828.

preservation of their [the seamen's] health."* Hammocks solved many of the problems raised by the enormous expansion of armaments on seventeenth- and eighteenth-century warships. Here is an eighteenth-century account given by William Falconer in his *Universal Dictionary of the Marine*, published in 1771.

As the management of the artillery in a vessel of war requires a considerable number of men, it is evident that the officers and sailors must be restrained to a narrow space in their usual habitations in order to preserve the internal regularity of the ship. Hence the 'hammocs,' or hanging beds of the latter are crowded together as close as possible between the decks, each of them being limited to the breadth of 14 inches. They are hung parallel to each other in rows, stretching from one side of the ship to the other nearly throughout her whole length, so as to admit of no passage but by stooping beneath them.
. . . As the cannon, therefore, cannot be worked while the hammocs are suspended in this situation, it becomes necessary (in an engagement) to remove them as quickly as possible. By this circumstance a double advantage is obtained, the batteries of cannon are immediately cleared of an encumbrance, and the hammocs are converted into a sort of parapet to prevent the execution of small shot on the quarter-deck, tops, and forecastle. At the summons of the boatswain, "Up all hammocs!" every sailor repairs to his own, and having stowed his bedding properly, he "cords" it up firmly

*M. Oppenheim, *A History of the Administration of the Royal Navy 1509–1660*, London, 1896.

with a lashing or line provided for that purpose. He then carries it to the quarter-deck, poop, or forecastle, or wherever may be necessary. As each side of the quarter-deck and poop is furnished with a double network, supported by iron cranes fixed immediately above the gunnel or top of the ship's side, the hammocs thus corded are firmly stowed by the quarter-master between the two parts of the netting so as to form an excellent barrier. The tops, waist, and forecastle are then fenced in the same manner.

And so the hammock allowed these great three-deckers to sleep eight hundred men and yet clear instantly for action, with the added bonus of providing protection from small-arms fire. Wooden berths, besides the weight and obstruction, would have splintered dangerously if the ship took enemy fire. Furthermore, the hammocks were sanitary. They were washed every week and hung from the mast to dry, eliminating problems with vermin. And how easy it was to get a lazy sailor on deck: a swift cut at the hammock lashing could end the deepest sleep.

But fourteen inches per man! This was common in Lord Nelson's time. Some ships afforded sixteen inches and petty officers were allowed all of two feet. Sometimes they slept in different shifts, but often enough they all had to sleep on their sides and woe to the man who wanted to turn over. Can you imagine what this was like on the lower deck, becalmed, during a Mediterranean or Caribbean summer, especially after a ration of the King's rum?

The hammock also served as a shroud. The dead seaman was sewn into his hammock and weighted with shot, and then dumped over the side with appropriate ceremony.

All European navies used hammocks. The French sometimes called them "hamac", but prefered "branle", derived from the swinging motion. The French equivalent of "Up all hammocks!", meaning stow them in preparation for action, was "Branles-bas!" The Dutch command was "Hangmatten af!" or "Hangmatten los!"

The British naval hammock is included in this book more because of its simplicity and historical interest than its beauty or comfort. Naval duty did not earn the hammock its reputation for luxury.

Late in the nineteenth century, more comfortable hammocks were imported to Europe and the United States from Brazil and Mexico. Hammocks became a minor fad before the First World War. I have a nostalgic image of the Good Old Days, a Golden Age of Hammocks, when free time was spent sitting around on front porches, the women in white linen dresses, the men wearing straw hats and striped blazers. It seems there are not so many hammocks around now as then and perhaps something has been lost: some understanding of how to savor leisure. For what is the ultimate symbol of relaxation but a hammock — with a pillow, a fan and a cold drink?

Dennis the Menace is at his worst when Mr. Wilson is in a hammock. How often has The Captain been blasted out of his hammock by the giant firecrackers of the Katzenjammer Kids? In how many cartoons of domestic life have you seen the hammock set in opposition to duty, as symbolized by the lawnmower?

I believe we need more hammocks, indoors and out. The gentle rocking motion seems to calm one down, like being cradled as a baby. What might hammocks do for the nation's temperament? Should psychiatrists replace the couch with a hammock? Should keyed-up executives relax in a hammock instead of a hotel? Could Mother's Hammock Hour add a new dimension to housework? Could workers take a hammock-break? Can the hammock usher in an Era of Tranquillity?

Drawing by George Price: © 1950 The New Yorker Magazine Inc.

The Mayan Hammock of Yucatan: A Tribute

Instructions on how to make a Mayan hammock would be too complicated for this book, but to write about hammocks without paying special attention to this particular type would be like writing about the world's cuisine and ignoring the French. The Maya of Yucatan, in southern Mexico, have brought hammock-making to the highest state of the art. They are also the greatest devotees of the hammock: in their legend the hammock is the gift of the gods.

Not too long ago, when hammocks were almost all made to satisfy local needs, many of the Mayan hammocks were made out of sisal. The fibers were rubbed almost endlessly against the worker's thighs until they were soft. It was believed that evil spirits entered the fiber from the thigh and to remove them a stool had to be rolled in the hammock before anyone used it. Now almost all hammocks are made of cotton and the evil spirits either stay in the thighs of the Mayans or are imported to New York. Each hammock is a giant net made of hundreds of thin cotton strands. There are no knots except at the ends. The weave looks a lot like the sprang weave, but is far more delicate. This web of fine cotton molds itself to the contours of your body. It is as close to flying as you can get without jumping out of an airplane.

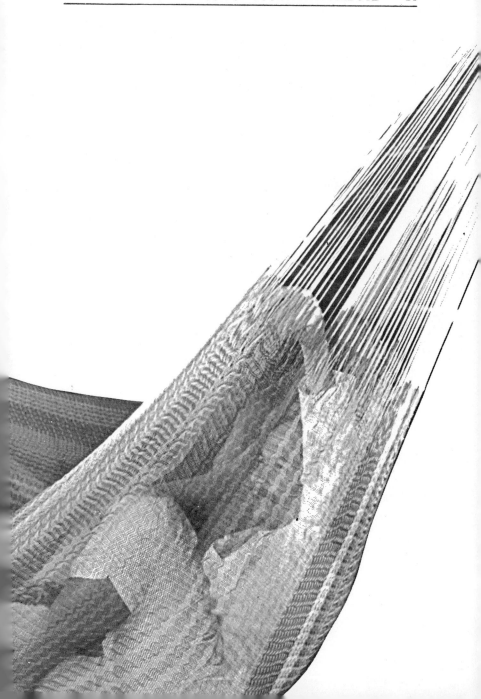

The young Mayan is born in a hammock. One prominent Yucatan midwife, Julia Santos, claims to have delivered three thousand babies in fifteen years, every one in a hammock. Babies sleep in hammocks with the edges tied together above them, forming a sort of cocoon. Children have bigger hammocks, single adults have larger ones yet, and when the Mayans marry, they move into the *matrimonial*, a hammock twelve feet across that can sleep two in completely separate pockets. Not necessarily separately, of course — contrary to our popular belief, the hammock is not a primitive form of birth control. In some remote parts of southern Mexico, in Chiapas, people are even buried in their hammocks.

The hammock is the only way to sleep in the extremely hot climate of Yucatan because any breeze blows not only around it but through it. Mosquito netting adds further protection for the sleeper. The poorer Mayans have no other important furniture except a table and a few stools. The hammock is their bed, easy chair and couch. Our sort of bed is apt to be a status symbol but any Mayan with any sense uses his hammock — and they are not afflicted with any special spinal curvature or defects. Hooks for hammocks are found all over their huts. When they visit relatives, they bring their own hammocks. Even the homes of wealthy Mayans have several hooks in all their rooms, including kitchens and hallways so that lots of relatives can be accommodated. Expensive hotels in Yucatan have hooks in the rooms for guests who prefer to bring their own hammock. Even the *matrimonial* weighs only about five pounds and folds up to the size of a loaf of bread.

The *matrimonial* takes two or three weeks to

make. Mayans start weaving at about eight years old. Most, but by no means all, of the weaving is done by women. Men tie on the white arms of the harness, a delicate art essential to a well-balanced hammock. The basic weave of some of the exported hammocks is made in the local jails by bad guys and even young Americans who got in trouble with the *federales* because of their fondness for certain of the local flora.

Exporting has recently turned the hammock into a cottage industry rather than a purely domestic art. This has not hurt the quality at all. In fact, better cotton has improved it and the colors for the American market are much more interesting than the off-whites and pinks preferred by the Mayans.

Are the Mayans exploited? This is a difficult question. Hammock-making is tedious work. The Mayans are very poor and their hammocks sell for a lot more in the United States than they do in Mérida, the capital of Yucatan. But this does reflect the unavoidable expenses of importing and marketing goods. I am certain that no one is getting rich from Mayan hammocks. Before large-scale American importing of hammocks, Mayan women would sell hammocks in the streets of Mérida for whatever they could get. Now they have a steady and sure market. I don't believe the hammocks could sell at higher prices, and if they did, it would probably pay someone to build a machine that did most of the work. Without this curious little industry, more Mayans would have to leave their villages and culture and go to work in the cities. It is hard to evaluate this or to suggest changes that would not do as much harm as good.

In buying a Mayan hammock, look for the following things:

1. See that the sides don't flop down when the hammock is hung; this would mean that the arms (the white harness string) have not been put on carefully.
2. Twist one of the arms between your fingers: if it unravels very easily, it may indicate an inferior cotton, likely to break.
3. See that the knots are at the ends of the hammock rather than in the main weave; this is just sloppy detail.

Cotton is king. I strongly advise against silky synthetics. They are hot, they tend to make you slide around to parts of the hammock you don't want to be in, they often lose their shape, they don't have class. Avoid cheap mail-order hammocks that look like the Mayan ones but aren't. Hammocks from other parts of Mexico are usually crude and are not made by Mayans. The Rolls Royce of all hammocks is the Mayan *matrimonial,* made of a special polished cotton called *ciguena* that looks at first glance like a synthetic but is not. Its colors are very bright and it holds them longer than other cottons and is especially strong.

Always back into a Mayan hammock and sit down in it, then put some material over your head and flop back, drawing your feet in after you. The hammock has no spreader; you open it with your body. You lie *across* it! If you want to sleep, place yourself diagonally in the hammock, never straight the long way as in other hammocks.

If you can't get down to Mérida, you can order directly from two places. They are:

Hammock Master, P.O. Box 354, Miami, Florida 33143, which will send you a multicolor *matrimonial* for seventy-five dollars and has a supply of the wonderful *cigueña* at one hundred dollars, and

The Hammock Way. Ghirardelli Square, San

Francisco, California 94109. Their brochure includes several kinds of hammocks, including the Brazilian hammock featured in this book.

The Brazilian Hammock

There may have been childhood experiences, but I can't remember. To the best of my knowledge, the first hammock came into my life only seven years ago. It was one of those hammock idylls: the fresh air of way-off rural New England, a warm spring day, the drone of bees, melodies of birds, the smells of fresh new grass and an orchard in bloom, the brightly striped hammock between two plum trees, rocked gently by a breeze that sighed in the nearby forest. Deep in the hammock, I drifted as in a trance, neither asleep nor awake, dreaming, completely relaxed, completely at rest with myself and the world.

My host told me he had bought the hammock at a New York department store. Of course, I determined to get one as soon as possible. But whenever I was in the confusion of New York, I did not think of hammock pastorals. The hammock in the warm fresh air of a spring day was like a beautiful dream of a former life.

I wanted a hammock made out of a single piece of material. The simple piece of canvas with reinforced or metal eyes at each end (described in the next chapter) is fine for nautical buffs, but I wanted something fancier. I saw some fabric hammocks in the Harvard Museum, examples of South American

Indian craft. They were fringed, like my first hammock of that New England spring. In fact, they looked a whole lot like it. Out to see my rural friends: yes, they still had the hammock. This time, how different from the first! Searching with a flashlight through a New England barn in the menacing early December dusk, shivering with cold, looking over old stalls and stanchions, rusty obsolete farm equipment, dusty hay bails, antique steamer trunks, and, finally, when chill was surpassing hope, the tangled hammock among cobwebs on a shelf. Later, unfolding it before a warm fire, I witness again the mutability of all things. The hammock, this symbol of springtime, faded, covered all over with dark mildew spots, lifeless, limp, a casualty of winter and neglect and time, yet, on close examination, still beautiful. A tag said it had been made in Brazil; certainly a close descendant of the ones in the museum. I saw I could duplicate it, making a few improvements in the harness at each end. Here it is. There is nothing very tricky about it. It takes time. But find a warm spring afternoon, and soft breeze and bees and birds, and my idyll will be yours.

Overview

Your first and most important task will be to select your fabric with care. (Details of buying cloth and construction follow.) Next, you indulge your fancy in all manner of gimcracks and gewgaws at a sewing or some similar shop. Your concern is decoration rather than weaving. If either edge needs hemming, now is the time. This is the simplest job with a sewing machine and very tedious without — something that should be kept in mind when you buy the fabric. Next, pull out enough weft strands to make three weftless stripes at each end of your fabric. The weft runs across the narrow width of the fabric; the warp the length of it. You will fold each end over right across the largest weftless stripe and sew it securely with strong thread, then gather the loose warp strands of the other stripes into small bunches to make a pattern across the width of the fabric, held in place by a strip of soutache, or some sort of ribbon. Then you will create two harnesses (hammock clews) out of clothesline by a clever braiding process, and attach them to the hammock. Finally, you will sew on the fringe, tassels or other nonsense that amuses you, put the hammock up, make a few adjustments and wait for birds, bees, a warm spring day, etc.

Nothing in this project is difficult in the sense that you might make some terrible error and ruin everything. Most of the work is a pleasant way to pass time and some of it is really interesting. Sewing by hand is tedious but requires no special knowledge. A machine can do all the sewing on this hammock in a half hour (surely you know someone with a machine) and all you have to know about a sewing machine for this project is how to thread it, how to make it go and how to make it stop. I hope no one in this day and age believes a project which requires sewing is for women only, involving some natural, inherited characteristic, like rhythm. Think of sailmaking!

Materials

"Luxury linen, Belgian linen or other upholstery fabric. 4½-5 feet by 8 feet. $12 and up.
Soutache, gimp or similar. 24 feet. Prices vary.
Fringe, tassels, etc. 6 yards altogether. Prices vary.
Braided clothesline. 200 feet, No. 6 or No. 7. $5 to $6.
Thread. Match it with the fabric and/or trim. If you plan to sew by hand, get button thread.
Sturdy needle or sewing machine.
Nail scissors and cheap utility scissors.
Measuring tape or stick.
String. 40 feet. No. 36 seine twine. (No. 21 cable cord, or anything similar.)

Making the Hammock

Section 1: Buying Material.

I have best luck in a city garment district where there are several competing shops dealing in upholstery fabric. Also, the Calico Corner chain offers a good selection of seconds. Prices vary enormously. I have found perfect material at four dollars a yard. Make that your target; you could pay twice as much. The fabric should be heavy and strong as for upholstery. It also should be loosely enough woven so that you can get a needle under one of the strands and pick out a loop of it as in a burlap-type weave. You will be pulling out several of the weft strands altogether. The best width is fifty-four inches; sixty inches is acceptable, forty-eight inches is getting a bit slim. Fabric comes with a tightly woven edge which won't unravel, called the selvage. If you buy material the correct width, with a selvage at both sides, you won't have to hem it later. Get three yards and trim a foot off or have the clerk do it carefully at the store.

Next, go to the biggest sewing, thread and button shop you can find. Buy some ribbon-type material to be woven across the hammock. Soutache is a sturdy, cheap, narrow braid that works fine for this but you may find something more handsome with similar properties you prefer. Select colors that will contrast nicely with your main fabric. Then buy the trim: fringe, tassels, puff-balls, tiebacks anything you want. You will be amazed at the variety of trim available at a wide range of prices. The Brazilian hammock has a simple string macrame trim and it is my heresy to find many machine-made trims more attractive. If you seek pure authenticity, you're on your own and good luck.

While you are at the sewing shop, pick up a spool of thread that matches the fabric. You may also want one that matches the trim. If you are going to sew by hand, use button thread for extra strength.

Section 2: If Necessary, Make a Hem.

Don't worry about the ends of the hammock now. This section is only in case you have a nonselvage edge (down the long side of your fabric) and is to prevent unraveling. Make sure the edge is cut straight. Fold the edge half an inch. Iron it flat. Fold it again half an inch so that the edge is completely buried inside the two folds. Iron. While you are doing this, you might as well get one side of the trim out of the way so sew it on, too. The side on which the hem shows will probably be the bottom. The trim will hang down whether it is on the top or the bottom so it is a matter of choice depending on whether or not you want the edge of the trim to show. This is an elaborate way of saying "do it any way you want." Do not attach trim to the last five and a half inches of fabric at either end. If you sew by hand, use a heavy needle to get through the three layers of fabric and the edge of the trim. Make a simple running stitch of a quarter inch the length of the hem, twice if you are a glutton for work, three times if you are serving a long jail sentence. One pass is sufficient with a sewing machine. Since you have had to make a hem along one edge, you should make a simple hem on the other (selvage) edge just for appearance.

Section 3: Pull out Weft Strands.

The weft strands run horizontally, across the fabric the short way. Pull out all the strands in a three-inch area, starting two and a half inches from the top, keep the next inch and a quarter solid, then pull all the weft strands for the next inch and a quarter, keep the next inch and a quarter solid and then pull a final stripe of an inch and a quarter. Turn the hammock around and do the same at the other end.

Removing weft strands is a challenge and a thrill to people who like dismantling things. I tried using a darning needle for a while, working out each strand an inch at a time, but it took forever. The tools that finally worked best for me were nail scis-

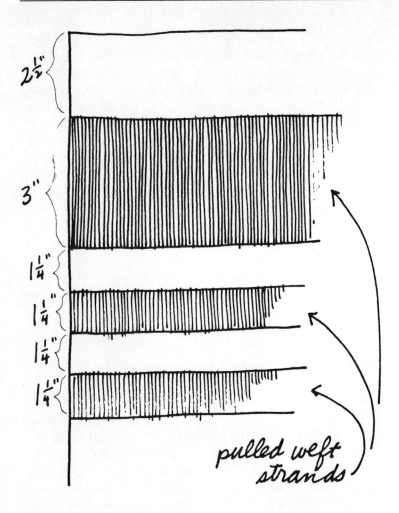

$2\frac{1}{2}''$

$3''$

$1\frac{1}{4}''$

$1\frac{1}{4}''$

$1\frac{1}{4}''$

$1\frac{1}{4}''$

pulled weft strands

sors and the pointed blade of a pair of cheap utility scissors. You might figure out something better.

Make sure the top and bottom of the fabric are cut as straight across as possible. A few strands may unravel as you work, no matter. Mark where the

weftless rows will be at one edge. Keeping the selvage or hemmed edge intact (that is, beginning at
about half an inch in from the edge) use the nail scissors to cut through the weft strands in the top
marked area. Be careful not to cut the warp (up and
down) strands, but if you nick one occasionally, it's
no disaster. Now trace the topmost cut weft strand
an inch across the hammock, reach under it with the
pointy scissor blade and pull that inch out. Keep
working along that row all the way to the other edge,
stopping where the selvage or hem begins. As you
work, cut the freed weft strand whenever it becomes
a nuisance. Go back and remove the bottom weft
strand from the same band. Now that the two miss-
ing rows mark the width of the band, carefully cut
through all the weft strands in between, at intervals
of about a foot across the entire band, and work the
rest of the weft strands out. The first couple of rows
may require the help of the scissor blade. After that,
the whole area should loosen up. You will be able to
work an inch of the strand out with your scissor
blade and pull the rest with a tug of your fingers. In
this way remove the weft from all six areas. It helps
a lot to be in a good light with the fabric resting on
something solid and flat of a contrasting color. I find
this oddly satisfying work.

Section 4: Weave the Loose Warp Strands into X's, Held in Place by a Strip of Soutache.

Sew a strip of soutache (or whatever you chose), a
few inches longer than the width of the hammock, to
the middle of the left edge of one of the weftless
inch-and-a-quarter bands. You could tie it around

the selvage or hem, but that's a bit sloppy. Now think of the warp strands in that band as being a continuous row of quarter-inch wide bunches. Call the first quarter inch of strands "bunch 1", the second quarter inch "bunch 2", etc.

$\frac{1}{4}''$ bundles

Essentially, you will loop each bunch through another bunch three places over to the right and hold them in a crossed position with the soutache.

Take bunch 4, pass it in front of bunch 3 and bunch
2. Take bunch 1 and tuck it under and through
bunch 4 with a little loop coming out the other side.
Put the other end of the soutache through this loop
and pull it through, thus holding bunches 1 and 4
together. Ignore bunch 2 — this is an irregularity at
the start of the row only. Bring bunch 6 in front of
bunch 5 and loop bunch 3 through it, running the
soutache through the loop of 3. Pass 7, join 8 and 5,
pass 9, join 10 and 7, pass 11, join 12 and 9. To show
you the pattern, the following bunches are joined:

1 and **4**
2 and nothing
3 and **6**
5 and **8**
7 and **10**
9 and **12**

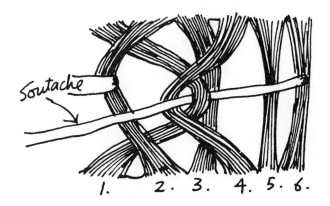

Join them all the way to the other edge where another bunch will probably be left out like bunch 2. Allow just enough soutache so that the hammock fabric lies open its full width without being gathered and sew it or tie it off at the far edge. Do this for all four inch-and-a-quarter bands, not for the wide two-and-a-half-inch bands.

Section 5: Secure the Two Ends.

Be sure the ends are cut straight and trim off any

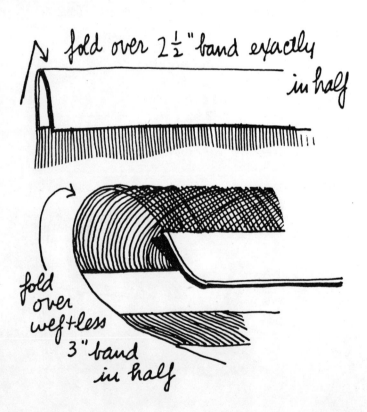

fold over 2½" band exactly in half

fold over weft+less 3" band in half

unraveled threads. Fold the solid top two-and-a-half
inches neatly in half. Run an iron over it to hold the
crease. Now fold it again right in the middle of the
weftless three-inch band, bringing the folded top directly in line with the first inch-and-a-quarter solid
portion. The loops of the folded weftless band will be
used later to attach the hammock to its harness.

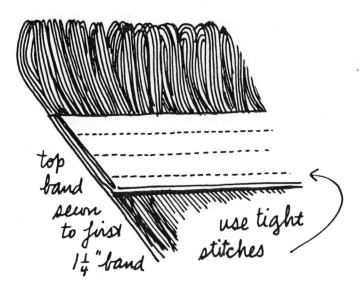

top
band
sewn
to first
1¼" band

use tight
stitches

Sometimes you may also have to iron that first
inch-and-a-quarter band because ironing stretches
some material and the top may overlap an inch or
two. Sew the top and the first inch-and-a-quarter
band together with three rows of tight stitches using
button thread.

Section 6: Make the Harness Loops.

This photograph from the National Maritime Museum (England) is a beautiful example of a harness or hammock clew. It has twenty-four ropes on it, a few more than we need. Start with ten ropes, each nine feet long, and put them around a coat hook or peg. Pull the ropes until they are the same length on each side of the peg; a difference of an inch or two between individual ropes does not matter. Gather the ropes into two tight bunches just below the peg. Tie a twenty-foot piece of string (No. 36 seine twine, No. 21 cable cord or anything similar) as tightly as you can around the left-hand bunch about four inches below the peg. Wind the string once around the right-hand bunch, also four inches below the peg, and then start winding the string around and around up the left-hand bunch only, pulling it tight each time around and pressing each row snugly against the one below. After a few turns around, you can take the ropes off the peg and work comfortably in your lap. As you go around the bend at the top where the peg was, you will have to overlap a few strings on the inside of the loop. Make sure the ropes are in a tight bunch when you come down the right side of the loop by pulling any slack ropes down through the single string you wound around them at the start. When you get to the bottom of the loop at the right side, wind the string a few times around *both* bunches together, then go between the two bunches and wrap the string a few times around the strings with which you just joined them, always keeping the string good and tight. Tie it off. Make another loop for the other end of the hammock.

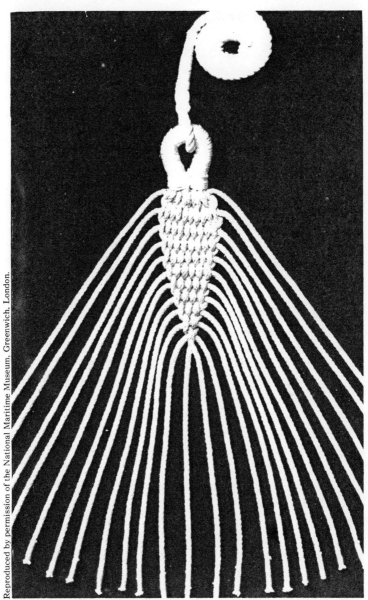

Reproduced by permission of the National Maritime Museum, Greenwich, London.

Section 7: Braid the Harnesses.

Hammer three long nails into a wall, about chest high, or find three coat hooks or similar projections. Put the loop on the middle one. Divide the ropes into a "front" ten and a "back" ten, taking five from each side of the loop for each rank. Separate the front and back rows by putting your left hand between them. (If you are left-handed, you may be more comfortable by reversing left and right in all the following instructions.) Starting at the right side, move the far right front strand to the back and bring the far right back strand to the front. Hold the ropes in their new position by putting the fingers of your right hand between them. Work your way across the row from right to left, bringing the front row to the back and the back row to the front and keeping the ropes separate by loading them onto your right hand. Always alternate front and back. When all the strands have been crossed over and are being held in position on your right hand, take the rope that is farthest to the right, pass it through the ropes, where your right hand is holding the rows apart, out at the left side and drape it over the nail located on that side. Take the farthest left rope and do the same, passing it between the rows and draping it over the nail on the right side. One of these ropes should be from the front row and the other from the back. Repeat this whole procedure with the remaining eighteen ropes, "weaving" the front ropes to the back and the back to the front, always alternating them and keeping them separate by putting them on the fingers of your right hand. (Keep each row in its original order; sometimes the ropes cross over in back and confuse you.)

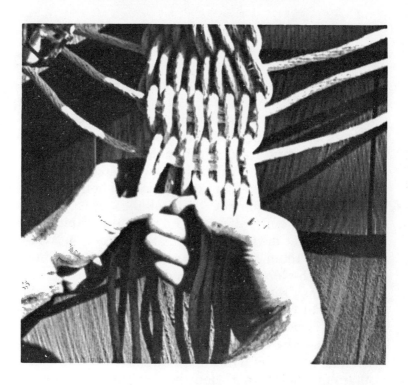

As you work, keep nudging the two ropes that passed through the rows up toward the loop. When all the ropes have been put on your right hand and the back row is now the front and the front row is now the back, move the new far left rope and the new far right rope through the rows and drape them out of the way on the nails as you did the previous two. Repeat again with the remaining sixteen ropes, nudging those that have been crossed over before up toward the loop. Continue working in this way, "weaving" the ropes back and forth and threading the two end ropes through until you have only two ropes left. Knot these together.

Section 8: Twist the Warp Strands That Are Now at the Ends of the Hammock.

Since you are going to attach the end strands to the harnesses, it is better to twist them together into stronger units. Consider the loose strands to be a row of quarter-inch bunches as in Section 4. Take bunch 1 in one hand and bunch 2 in the other and roll the threads between thumb and fingers, rolling each bunch in the same direction. When they are tightly rolled, line the two bunches up alongside each other and roll them both together into one bunch, this time rolling in the other direction. When you have them as tight as you can, hook a finger through the loop and tug good and hard. Work your way across the entire top and bottom. Most of the loops will come unwound to some extent, depending, in part, on the type of fabric. A few may come unwound altogether. This is no problem because enough of a twist will remain in most loops to make them much stronger than they would have been as individual strands.

Section 9: Attach the Harness.

First practice this bowline knot:

Make a loop. Run the end of your rope through the loop thereby making a new loop underneath. Go around the rope just above the first loop and return back through the first loop again. Pull tight, preserving the second loop. Or, as they say in the Scouts, up the rabbit hole, around the tree and back down the rabbit hole again. Anyway, it is very handy

for tying up your yacht and, along with a square knot or whatever it is that children get in their shoelaces, it should be all the nautical lore you need.

Divide the end loops roughly equally among the ropes of the harness. Use the bowline knot putting

the bottom (second) loop of the bowline through the hammock loops. Make all the harness ropes about the same length, allowing an extra couple of inches toward the middle. Leave an extra ten inches of rope after each bowline so you can make adjustments.

Section 10: Sew on the Trimming.

Put the trim on whichever side looks best to you; it will hang down in either case. This hammock does not have a top or a bottom unless you so determine because of a hem or sloppy stitches on one side. Trim on the side of the "occupant" is vulnerable unless tightly sewn.

Section 11: Lie in It.

Install your hammock as described in the last chapter of the book. Tie-ropes allow you to vary the bow of the hammock to taste. Adjust harness ropes for comfort and balance if necessary. Cramped shoulders means the outside ropes are too short. A ridge under you means the inside ropes should be longer. I wouldn't trim off excess rope until the hammock has been lolled in a good while. Got it right? Good! Now climb in (seat first, of course) with a pillow and a cold glass of sarsaparilla. Hell, make it a double! Think Spring.

The Naval Hammock

The Brazilian Hammock seems like a lot of work. Why not just buy a piece of canvas, sew a few seams, punch in some grommets, tie on the harness, climb in and snore? Why not indeed. This is by far the simplest hammock in the book, yet it is the only one that ever failed me. My first attempt sent me crashing to the floor in utter humiliation.

The problem, as it turned out, was not in the main body of the hammock itself, nor in the harness. The weakness was in fitting the two together. I had used metal eyelets purchased at a sewing shop for fifty cents a dozen, complete with an installing device. This is a bargain for making flags or deerskin jackets, but I would not put them in a hammock that was to hold over one hundred twenty pounds. A sailmaker taught me to use No. 1 burred grommets (metal eyes) and to install them with a grommet die, retailing at around fifteen dollars and a hole puncher which I could buy for another five dollars. To get around this expense, sailmakers, tentmakers, awning makers and some flag makers will install these grommets for you at twenty-five cents a piece, or ten dollars for the hammock. Perhaps you can do better. Another nuisance to have in mind before you attempt this hammock: like the Brazilian hammock, it is very easy with a sewing machine and quite a chore to sew by hand, however authentic.

Why bother with it at all? Two reasons: utility and romance. It is a tough and simple hammock, durable in salt air, easy to shorten to fit into a van or bus. It costs thirteen to fifteen dollars and is comfortable enough, although certainly the least comfortable hammock in the book.

Which brings me to romance: the sea, the bounding main. "Pipe all hands aboard, Mr. Christian." This hammock, with many subtle variations, has swung in the navies of Europe for over three hundred years. The idea was to put the most sailors in the least space. At one time, the canvas was only five feet long and each seaman was allowed fourteen

inches of lateral space. But those sailors and marines pretty much conquered the world, no easy achievement with a backache. Comfort was not a major consideration because the navy was so often the employer of last resort. When you went down to the docks in the evening for a few drinks and awoke the next morning as an enlisted man with a headache, it was not for you to be particular about the accommodations. But what does that matter when you are two days out of Liverpool, going to singe the Spanish King's beard?

Materials

Canvas. 6½ feet by 4 feet. You lose 6 inches of length in making the hammock. Make it a little longer for an extra tall occupant or a little shorter to fit into a van. The width can vary a few inches, too, preferably wider. Quality heavy canvas can cost as much as $3.00 a yard at an expensive fabric shop but should cost less if you hunt around.

Rope. 200 feet. I used No. 7 braided clothesline at $2.80 per 100 feet. A ⅜ inch polypropylene is handsomer but harder to tie.

Needle and strong thread. Or a sewing machine.

Grommets. Forty. No. 1 burred.

Grommet die.

Hole Cutter.

(Better yet for these last three items, the friendly services of 1) a sailmaker 2) a tentmaker 3) an awning maker or 4) [maybe] a flag maker.)

Making the Hammock

Section 1: Make the Main Body of the Hammock.

Detailed sewing instructions were given with the Brazilian hammock. These will be brief and should suffice because this hammock is so simple. Along the edges (lengthwise) turn the canvas one-half inch and sew a seam. At each end (across the width), fold the canvas over an inch and a half, press it with an iron, fold it again another inch and a half and iron it again. The ends of the hammock will be three layers thick, one and a half inches wide. Sew two or three rows of stitches, none closer than an inch from the ends so there is plenty of room for the grommets. Then make twenty evenly spaced marks locating the grommets in these thick portions at each end of the canvas. It is very easy to make mistakes placing these holes, so do not mark with ink or anything you wouldn't want to show until you are certain. Install (or have installed) the grommets.

Section 2: Make the Harnesses.

The harness for the Brazilian hammock in the previous chapter was used in the British Navy. I recommend you use it, starting with ten ropes, each nine feet long. The same harness, using a two-and-half-inch metal ring, described in the Twin Oaks hammock chapter, was also used at sea.

Section 3: Attach the Harnesses to the Hammock.

Use bowline knots as in the Brazilian hammock. The canvas hammock lacks flexibility, making it especially important that the harness ropes be the right length. I make the center ropes no more than two inches longer than the end ropes and let the others graduate bit by bit in between. If the ropes near the edges are too tight, your shoulders will feel pinched. If the middle ropes are too tight, they will carry too much weight and the canvas will form a ridge under your back. Make adjustments until it feels right.

Section 4: How to Lie in It.

Back in. Take a pillow with you. Be sure the hooks creak. Try saying a few things like, "Avast!" and "Land-Ho!" Drink something with rum in it. At the cry of "Up all hammocks!" step lively at stowing yours and prepare to give those Spaniards a taste of grapeshot.

The Twin Oaks Hammock

Twin Oaks is a ten-year-old commune of eighty members modeled loosely after B. F. Skinner's utopian novel *Walden Two*. And by golly, it works! This is a happy, stable, hard-working, well-organized group of (mostly) young people. They have built a comfortable noncompetitive society for themselves in rural Virginia, and are providing inspiration for similar communities by their example. The rootless members of our counter-culture are fortunate if they can find a life here, but only the more stable and truly committed can adjust to it.

Hammock-making is the principal industry at Twin Oaks. The members taught me their methods during a three-day visit, and I call this the Twin Oaks hammock to return their courtesy. Actually, this type has been made elsewhere for some time with slight variations; in particular, on Pauley's Island, South Carolina.

One of the biggest problems of any communal society is how to divide up the work. Twin Oaks has organized an elaborate system of labor credits wherein all the chores from answering mail to scrubbing pots are rated according to desirability.

One person is in charge of assigning work to all the members, making everything as fair and as close to each member's wishes as possible. The Hammock Manager tells the Labor Credit Manager how many people-hours are needed to meet the agreed quota and the Labor Credit Manager supplies the bodies. A member may find himself assigned to two or three hours of hammock work a day along with several hours of construction or kitchen duties. Varying jobs keeps anyone from feeling imprisoned by their work. Hammock-making is really pleasant, although too much of it can become monotonous. The shop is new, spacious and brightly lit with big windows. Eight people can be working on the basic weave of as many hammocks at the same time. There is a soothing rhythm to the work and a sense of ac-

Original Pauley's Island Hammock,
photo courtesy of The Hammock Way

complishment as the hammocks grow under the
shuttle. The members chat pleasantly with each
other (malicious gossip is forbidden at Twin Oaks)
or they wear one of the sets of headphones located at
each weaving position and listen to taped music.
How strange it is to see several people doing little
dances or breaking into odd snatches of song as they
work and not to hear the music that inspires such
behavior! The hammock shop, like everything else
at Twin Oaks, is always open and the members can
fulfill their obligations at any time of day or night, an
hour or two here and there.

A hammock can be manufactured in four to six
hours. Selling at wholesale, the commune realizes
about three dollars per hour of work. Mail order
earns them about double. The address is Twin Oaks

Community, Louisa, Va. 23093. Their superb large hammock can be ordered for fifty-five dollars and is well worth it. They also produce a splendid hanging hammock chair for seventy-five dollars.

The hammocks at Twin Oaks are made from a wonderfully soft polypropylene rope. Instead of knots, pieces of rope are joined by melting the edges with a soldering iron and then pressing the melted portions together for a moment until they fuse. This rope is snow white, very light weight and will not mildew (a problem with cotton in only the most humid climates). Unfortunately, it is almost impossible to find. All the polypropylene I could locate in the Boston area was stiff, scratchy and too expensive. After a few telephone calls, I learned that all the soft polypropylene anyone knew about was the by-product of a rug manufacturer in North Carolina, and the entire supply was sent to Twin Oaks. Unless you are lucky enough to turn some of this rope up, use everyday cotton clothesline. It does have a more hand-craft look about it.

Photo courtesy of Twin Oaks

Overview

Here is what you will do. You will go to Sears or its equivalent and buy about twenty-three dollars' worth of clothesline and a few other odds and ends to be described later. You will have some wooden staves cut to order at a lumberyard and will hunt around for some metal rings. Next, you will make two chains out of rope to serve as the edges of the hammock. You will build a simple weaving frame out of two dowels and make your own shuttle. Following detailed instructions rather blindly, you will begin weaving the main body of the hammock. After a period of confusion and doubt, the netting pattern will emerge and you will get the happy feeling that you almost know what you are doing. You will still worry about small mistakes and may have to redo a row from time to time, but by following a simple formula, work will proceed rapidly, giving you increasing satisfaction. Then you will drill holes in the staves, making the spreaders that hold the hammock open. You will create a harness for each end, a neat trick in itself, attach the harness to the spreader and, finally, to the main body of the hammock. During this entire process, you will never really know what a grand object you are creating. The moment you have it up and actually lie in it, you will realize that it worked and actually is far more beautiful than you had hoped. This Achievement-Despite-Great-Obstacles high will last for days. Your friends will grow tired of hearing about it. But any time you want to feel good about yourself, you can go lie in your hammock.

Materials

Clothesline. 900 feet. Braided cotton No. 6. Comes in two 100-foot hanks joined together. At Sears, about $2.80 per 100 feet.

Dowels (round sticks). Two. 1 inch diameter. 3 or 4 feet long. Sears or any hardware store. About 80¢ each. Old broom handles could do.

Staves. Two. 1" × 1" × 65". Hardwood, like oak. $2.00 to $5.00 at a lumberyard depending on luck, minimum milling charge, etc. Read carefully Section 9, "Prepare the Spreaders," for further instructions before making a purchase.

Metal rings. Two. 2½-inch diameter. Cadmium or zinc coated is the best but not essential. Available at large hardware stores or marine supplies stores.

Scrap of beaverboard or plywood or equivalent. See Section 3, "Make Your Shuttle," for details.

Measuring tape. 8 feet or more is ideal.

Nails. One 6 to 8 inches. Several 2 inches.

Tin or plastic cup. See Section 10, "Make the Harness," for details.

Sandpaper. One sheet. Medium.

Adhesive tape. White, ½ inch. Optional.

Hammer. Electric drill. Chisel. Worry about these when you come to them.

Photo courtesy of Twin Oaks

Making the Hammock

Section 1: Make the Edge of the Hammock.

Each edge is a rope chain, seventy-eight inches long. Start with a twenty-eight-foot length of rope. Tie a bowline (see page 45 in the chapter on the Brazilian hammock) in one end and pull it tight, making sure the loop at the bottom is about as big as a silver dollar and leaving a little tail at the end, one and a half inches long or longer. Make a loop in the rope immediately next to the knot and put it through the large loop of the bowline until it protrudes about an inch and a quarter to one inch and a half. Make another loop with the next portion of rope and put that through the previous one, thereby making a chain. Use the same motion in making each link of the chain. If you are unhappy with your work, tug on

the unused portion of rope and it will unravel all the way back to the bowline. When there is about a foot of rope left, stretch the chain lightly and add or subtract links until it is seventy-eight inches long. Make the last link silver dollar size. Wrap the rope around the next to last link, go through that link, then through the loop you just made by wrapping the rope around, and pull it tight. Tug on the final loop to make sure it is secure. Make the other edge chain as much like the first as you can. One more or one less link or inch really won't matter, except to the perfectionist. When you are satisfied, cut off all the extra rope leaving a small tail for security. With adhesive tape, bind all the tails alongside the final loops to make things neater. If you accomplish nothing else with this project, you will love your chains.

Section 2: Build the Weaving Frame.

Take two one-inch dowels, each three or four feet long, and make a notch in one end of each so that a piece of rope can be wedged in and held securely. What a simple instruction! For me this was the hardest part of making my first hammock and I have the scars to prove it. My solution was to use a hammer and chisel to start a notch, split the dowel a little ways past that and then bind it up with tape so it didn't break altogether. You're on your own.

Next, explore your house with a measuring tape. Find a place where the dowels can be affixed (hammered in) to stand upright so that the tops are seventy to seventy-two inches apart. Have the dowels angle gently towards each other so that there is a little more distance between them below the top,

and have them angled away from any wall, door jamb or post they may be attached to so that they are clear enough to allow ropes to slide up and down the top eighteen inches or more. It is perfectly all right if the dowels are at odd angles to each other. The slots in each dowel should be pointed generally toward the other, and the tops of the dowels should be about chest high to allow you to work comfortably.

Measure from the top of the left dowel to the top of the right. Measure beyond the right dowel far enough to *total* eighty-four inches. Make a clear mark at that place or, if for some reason you can't, make your mark the appropriate number of inches down the dowel itself. Now do the same going the other way: make a mark that locates the distance between the tops of the two dowels plus enough inches to make a total of eighty-four inches. Near the left dowel, display an arrow pointing up. At the right dowel, make an arrow pointing down. This will all make sense later.

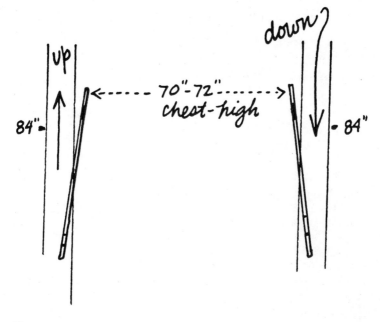

Summary:

1. Tops seventy to seventy-two inches apart.
2. Dowels leaning *generally* towards each other.
3. Eighteen or more inches of dowel available for use.
4. Tops about chest high.
5. Mark the eighty-four-inch points.
6. Display up and down arrows.

Section 3: Make Your Shuttle.

A shuttle is a device that holds two hundred feet of rope and allows you to move the whole bulk in and out of tight spaces with precision. The ideal design is about five inches wide, eighteen to twenty-four inches long, with plenty of room between the horns to load rope, a notch so you can begin winding the rope on easily and tapered ends so it can be worked through tight places.

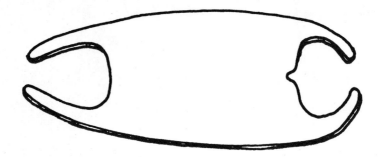

If you have a thin piece of wood and a coping saw or some Great Machine for cutting patterns of this sort, life is simple indeed. If not, it's Ingenuity Time again. I used a scrap of beaverboard, hacked the shape out with a hammer and chisel, fastened the horns on with heavy staples when they broke off, and did fine.

Section 4: Load the Shuttle.

The rope will probably come in two one hundred-foot hanks joined together. Don't cut them. Find a loose end, tie a simple knot and catch it in the notch of the shuttle. If you hold the shuttle in one hand and wind the rope around it with the other, you will create one twist every time around and this will plague you later (remember yo-yo's?). It is better to sort of juggle the hanks with your feet and wind the rope by turning the shuttle end over end with both hands, maintaining some tension as you do it. You should be able to wind all two hundred feet on the shuttle. At Twin Oaks, using the soft polypropylene, all the rope for a hammock is put on one shuttle allowing an uninterrupted weave. Of course, Twin Oaks is a utopian community.

Section 5: Put an Edge Chain on the Loom.

Examine the chain. You will notice a flat side and a side with bumps. You will also notice that one side of the links has a double strand of ropes and the other a single strand. Ideally, when the hammock is completed, the bumps will be on the under side and the double strand will be the outside edge. In fact, a departure from this ideal will hardly be noticed. Slip the end loops of the chain over the dowels. Get rid of any twists in the chain.

Section 6: Attach the Rope on the Shuttle to the Chain.

Unwind eight to ten feet of rope from the shuttle. Starting at the right-hand side, put the end of the rope through the second link of the chain (or the next link if that one is tightly closed up), looping it around the single strand edge. Then thread it through at fourteen *other* places (single strand edge if possible), ending with the last open link at the left side. Be sure the distance between each place is about equal, about every four or five links of chain. You will probably have to do it a few times to get it spaced right. Once you are satisfied that 1) the rope passes through the chain at fifteen places and 2) the places

15 places attached to rope chain

are evenly spaced, tie the end of the rope securely to the dowel above the chain's loop. Leave a little space next to the dowel when tying this and all knots so that a rope can be slipped through along the dowel later.

Section 7: Weave the Main Body of the Hammock.

Read this section through once completely, understanding whatever you can. Then proceed on faith, step by step.

Standing at the right-hand dowel pull the rope you have just passed through the chain (which is now tied to the left dowel) tight to the top of the right dowel. Pull it tight enough to have moderate tension, but not so tight as to risk snapping the left dowel. Tuck the shuttle under your left arm, hold the rope against the top of the dowel with your left hand and measure the rope out to your eighty-four-inch mark with your right hand, keeping the tension. Then relax the tension and wedge the rope, where it measured out to eighty-four inches, into the notch at the top of the right dowel. This is the point of the eighty-four-inch marks: no matter how much the angles of the dowels may vary, or which direction you are working in, or whatever the idiosyncrasies of your weaving, each row will be about eighty-four inches long. Once the row is wedged into the notch, run it around behind the dowel, check your arrow sign (pointing down) and stuff the shuttle *down* from the top of the right dowel through the first loop, the one you just made between the next to last link and a few links to the left. This may take some stuffing with a full shuttle. It will get easier soon. (If, somehow, the foot or so of slack is not enough, mark the eighty-four-inch point clearly on the rope, allow yourself some more slack, and restore the rope to the notch at the eighty-four-inch point before measuring at the left dowel.) Now push the shuttle *down* through the next loop and continue to the end until you have made *fourteen* "stuffs," always putting the shuttle down through the loops. Now that you are back at the left dowel, extend the rope under moderate tension to that eighty-four inch mark. Having measured it, back off and wedge the rope at eighty-four inches into the notch at the top of the left dowel. Bring the rope around behind the dowel. Check your arrow (up). Now work back to the right, *fourteen* passes in all, each time moving the shuttle *up* through the loop. Make your first pass after the first crossed-over ropes. Always be sure you are looping the rope around the row you just completed before. Give a tug with your free hand where you think the shuttle should go next. It should create a diamond shape with four corners, the fourth being where your hand is and there should not be a fourth rope or corner already there (if there is, it means you have grabbed on to a rope from a row before the most recent row).

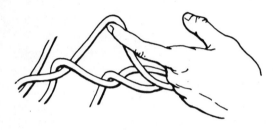

Your fourteen up passes will end near the right dowel. Measure out to the eighty-four-inch mark on the right dowel, remove the loop that is already in the notch there, drop it over the dowel and put the latest rope at its eighty-four-inch point in its place. Go behind the dowel, check your arrow (down), work back to the left making fourteen passes, starting after the first crossed ropes, looping only around rope from the previous row, measure the eighty-four-inch mark, drop the rope already in the notch over the dowel and wedge in the new, check your arrow (up), make fourteen passes, etc.

Summary:

1. Always alternate putting the shuttle up through the weave for an entire row and down for an entire row, according to your arrow.

2. Always make fourteen passes with each row. It is a good idea to count out loud, "up one, up two, up three . . . eighty-four inches, wedge, around, down one, down two, etc." If you come out with more or less than fourteen, it indicates that you have messed up. Stop at once, find your mistake, undo your weave back to the last row where you came out right, and proceed. The number fourteen is your only critic and guide.

3. Start each row after the first crossed-over rope of the previous row.

4. Check for a diamond shape before each pass. If you tug in the right place, you will open up an obvious hole for your shuttle.

5. Never have two ropes going together through the same corner of a diamond.

Consolation: the beginning of the body of the hammock is, psychologically, the worst part of the entire project. After a few rows, the shuttle will become smaller and easier to work with, the diamond pattern of the weave will become obvious, you will be sure about where to make each pass, you will gain speed and develop a pleasant rhythm, you will have a sense of competence and hope of eventual success. Keep struggling in your darkest moments. It builds character.

When you come to the end of the shuttle load, go back to the last complete eighty-four-inch row and tie it off at the dowel remembering, as always, to leave a little space in the tie-off loop. Reload the shuttle, tie the end on the dowel right over where you tied off the last row and continue as usual. Do not have any knots except at the ends of the hammock. Continue until you have forty loops around each dowel *in addition to* the two chain loops, the original tie-on loop and the final tie-off loop. Where you have tied off and tied on rope any place in the middle (because your shuttle ran out), those two loops together count as only one of the forty loops at that dowel. The final tie-off should be at the other dowel (right) from the first tie-on loop. In making that final row, proceed as follows:

Section 8: Attach the Other Chain to the Body of the Hammock.

Place the second chain over the dowels. Untwist it and, if possible, have the bumps facing the same way as the bumps on the first chain and have the single strand side of the chain on the bottom where it will receive the final row. Take enough rope off the shuttle to make an eighty-four-inch row as usual plus an extra foot so you can tie off. Weave the last row through the first available link of the chain, as you did at the beginning, and then through the appropriate loop of the last row of the hammock, going up or down, according to the arrow (ideally up — you should be going from left to right). Continue until you have made fourteen passes through the hammock and fourteen through the chain. Make a fifteenth pass through the chain at the last available link, measure out to eighty-four inches, and tie the rope off just under the chain loop. If, somehow, you end up with too many or too few rows, or if the final tie-off is on the same side as the first tie-on, or if the chain is twisted, you will still have a fine hammock.

On each dowel, run a rope through all the loops and tie its ends together. This is an extra safety measure to prevent loops from falling off the dowel when you move it, destroying the weave. Although you could remove the hammock from the dowels, relying solely on the safety rope, it is best to detach the dowels themselves from their standing position, keeping the hammock on them until it is time to attach the hammock to the harnesses.

Section 9: Prepare the Spreaders.

The purpose of the spreader is to hold the hammock open. Some hammocks are meant to envelop you. The Twin Oaks hammock is a flexible grid, acting more like a bed.

At Twin Oaks, the communards buy quantities of oak that is still green, trim it into $1'' \times 1'' \times 5'$-long staves and stack them under tension in wooden frames that bend them as they dry into a gentle bow of about two inches. The spreaders are then drilled in twenty-two places on a drill press, the holes are counter-sunk so that the ropes will not chafe against sharp edges. Finally, the spreaders are shellacked to protect them against the elements. That's first class but hard to arrange, especially in a city apartment. The bow is a good touch but not essential. You can bend dry staves by lying them across several pots of boiling water for five or six hours, putting cookie sheets over them to help the steam linger around, then stacking two bricks under the middle and putting a great weight at each end until they dry in two days. A bow of four inches will unbend back to two inches once the weights are removed. Personally, I would just as soon skip the whole process and settle for a straight spreader.

The Yellow Pages are full of lumberyards. At some, most of the customers are real carpenter-types with hammers and screwdrivers hanging all over their overalls. Ordering three dollars' worth of wood may seem like ordering one meatball at the Ritz. Don't be intimidated; most lumberyards sell all sorts of odds and ends to professionals and amateurs alike. It's a good idea to call first and ask if they have any hardwood, oak preferred.

You may have to buy an entire plank, ten foot by five inches by one and a quarter, and then have it milled to the right size. A rough one-and-a-quarter inch dresses down to a polished one inch. One inch dresses down to three-quarters of an inch, and that's getting a bit slender. As long as you are buying the whole board and paying a minimum milling charge, you might as well get some extra spreaders. Avoid knots; they are apt to be weak.

Drill twenty-two holes in each spreader, each hole large enough for the rope to pass through. I use a quarter-inch electric drill and widen the holes somewhat by wobbling the bit around after I have drilled each one. Space the holes evenly, try to drill through the middle of the stave, and break through to the other side gently to avoid splintering the wood. If you have a bowed spreader, drill through the side on which the spreader lies flat so that, when you lie in the hammock, the ends of the spreader will be higher than the middle. If you don't have an electric drill, don't worry. They are as common as electric razors. Ask your neighbor, building superintendent, gas station attendant, nearby school shop-teacher or anyone you know who is handy. Explain your problem — the Hammock Mystique makes people very friendly. If you have a countersink bit handy with the drill, it's a simple matter to countersink the holes (make them flare out near the surface). This is not essential, but it could prevent some wear on the ropes. Round off all the edges of the spreader with sandpaper. It is not essential, but if the hammock is going to stay outdoors in a lot of bad weather, it might be a good idea to coat the spreader with some kind of varnish. Consult your local hardware store. If children are going to play around the hammock, you would also be wise to pad the ends of the spreader with tape.

Section 10: Make the Harnesses.

Buy two two-and-a-half-inch metal rings, zinc or cadmium-coated preferred. They may be unavailable at smaller stores, and a telephone call could save you legwork. Find a plastic or metal cup, wider at the top than at the bottom, which fits easily through the ring, the ring wedging tightly somewhere between the cup's top and middle. Cut eleven lengths of rope, each one hundred twenty-five inches long. Loop them through the ring so that their ends are even. Hold the ropes in place with your finger and jam the cup through the ring as far as it can go so that all the ropes are held tightly in place, right next to each other, pressed between the cup and the ring. Hammer a six- to eight-inch nail in somewhere at about shoulder height, slanting it upward so that the cup can rest firmly on it and hammer in lesser nails on either side of this big nail, a few inches away from

Photo courtesy of Twin Oaks

it. If this is difficult you could make do with a row of three coathooks. Put the cup on the large nail or center coathook and let the ropes hang down. Now you have two rows of eleven strands each, a front row and a back row. You weave the ropes in the same manner as the harness of the Brazilian hammock. Starting at the right side, move the far right front strand to the back and bring the far right back strand to the front. Work your way across the row from right to left, bringing the front row to the back and the back row to the front, always alternating front and back and maintaining the original order of the strands. As you work, load the crossed-over strands onto your right hand to hold them in their new position and nudge them gently up against the ring. When all the strands have been crossed over and are being held in their new position by your right hand, take the farthest strand on the left side and the farthest on the right side and carry them through the ropes where your right hand is holding them apart so that they cross each other and come out on the other sides. Drape them out of the way over the nails conveniently placed on each side of them. Repeat the procedure with the remaining twenty strands, alternating front to back and then carrying the outer left and right strands through and draping them out of the way. Keep nudging the newly alternated ropes up against the ropes that just passed through the rows and nudge everything toward the ring. Be careful to select the strands in their original order: frequently they cross over each other in the back row and will fool you unless you examine each strand carefully before moving it. Continue in this way until only two strands remain. Tie these together up against the previously crossed-under strands with an ordinary square knot. The harness will look something like a bunch of grapes with twenty-two ropes hanging off it. Neat trick, wot? Now do it all again, to make the other harness.

Section 11: Attach the Spreader to the Harness.

Remove the cup and hang the ring over the large nail. Put the twenty-two ropes from the harness

Photo courtesy of Twin Oaks

through the corresponding twenty-two holes in the spreader and tie the simplest knot in the ropes at both ends so they won't slip back through the spreader. Leave a foot of rope after each knot. Push down on the spreader to see that it is not askew, that each end rope is the same length. Tie simple knots in all the other ropes. Check your work by pushing down on the spreader. All the ropes will not have the same tension, and you will have to untie and retie several knots. When you can push down on the spreader and all the ropes show some tension, none hanging slack, you are close enough. Be sure the spreader is not askew and that ten inches or more of rope hangs below each knot. Do the same to the other spreader.

Section 12: Attach the Harnesses to the Body of the Hammock.

Clear the room of noise and distraction. Control your trembling hands. This is an easy step but you can really mess things up if you lose track of what you are doing. I once almost ruined a hammock by going to answer the telephone. Place one end of the hammock next to a spreader. Look over the end of the hammock and see to it that all the loops are in order (this is easier if they are still on the dowel). If you made your chains well, the smooth side will be the top side of the hammock. Don't worry about it if this detail didn't work out. Untie the safety rope but leave it in place. Only remove those loops from the safety rope (and dowel) that you are about to tie onto the harness — the danger is that you can easily lose track of just what went around the dowel and what didn't. First, take the chain loop and attach it to the end harness rope. Make a bowline as close to the simple knot as you can. While making the bowline's second (bottom) loop, pass the rope through the chain's loop. Make a bowline in each harness rope, each time incorporating two loops off the dowel in the bottom loop of the bowline. Make the bottom loop about the size of a silver dollar so that the ropes can slide back and forth and adjust themselves. Include the first tie-on and the last tie-off loops with the two loops going on the second harness rope. Tie-on and tie-off loops in the middle of the hammock count as half a loop each. If, for any reason, you have miscounted, it is all right to have one loop or three loops attached to a harness rope. Remember, only take those loops off the safety rope that you are about to attach and attach them immediately. Tie the other chain loop onto the corresponding end harness rope. Do not cut off the extra bits of rope. You might want to make adjustments later, especially by lengthening the middle ropes an inch or two to make the hammock steadier. Attach the other harness to the hammock. If you are using bowed spreaders, be sure they both curve the same way.

Section 13: How to Lie in It.

Even at this point, the hammock looks like a pile of rope. Put up your hammock (see the last chapter on Installation). Isn't it glorious? Back into it, putting your seat near the middle. Flop back, spreadeagle, until you get your balance. Relax. Open a bottle of champagne. Then tell the world.

The Sprang Hammock

I decided to learn how to make a woven hammock that was truly "ethnic." The Twin Oaks hammock is the showboat of this book; I wanted something subtle, more artsy-craftsy, a hammock made for centuries by some ancient race in a remote land. Inquiries brought me to Joanne Segal Brandford, Radcliffe Institute Fellow in the area of fabric design and weaving techniques. Ms. Brandford showed me the sprang hammock and it was just what I wanted: images of loin-clothed natives deftly twisting strands outside their adobe huts danced before me. I was referred to a student for lessons and an unpublished M.A. thesis for background. The thesis writer described the technique as follows, "a form of weftless finger-weave in which the strands are manipulated while in a stretched position. Consecutive pairs, or groups, of warps are continuously twisted around each other to form rows of hexagonal meshes. A further characteristic of this technique is the duplication in reverse of each row of twists at the upper end of the warp skein."* Nothing could be simpler unless, like myself at the start of this project, you do not know a warp from a weft and think a

*Irmgard Weitlaner-Johnson. Twine-Plaiting: A Historical, Technical and Comparative Study. (unpublished M.A. thesis, University of California, August 1950). All subsequent historical information was gleaned from this excellent paper.

shuttle is a train you catch at Times Square. To make everything perfectly clear: the warp is made of the vertical strands and the weft of the horizontal. In true weaving, the warp and the weft are interlaced to make fabric. In sprang, there is no weft, just warp strands twisted together to create a net-like effect.

Sprang is an ancient method of making material, perhaps a predecessor of true weaving. Historians have a problem with what to name which technique because of the infinite small variations. The author I just quoted calls it "twine-plaiting," but plaiting usually means braiding, and more recent classifications prefer to call it "sprang." Sprang, or work similar to sprang is also sometimes called "Egyptian plaiting," "Coptic lace," and, mistakenly, "knotless netting." Some of the best prehistoric sprang finds have turned up in Denmark where late Bronze Age (1,500 B.C.) discoveries include a hair-net, a sash, and a cap. Called by the Vikings in the ninth century "spräng väy," it reached its highest development in Norway in the eighteenth century in the manufacture of towels, mittens, caps, and garters. In parallel development, evidence of the technique has been found in southern Italy from 300 B.C.; sprang was used in Coptic Egypt in the third to ninth centuries A.D., primarily for caps and shawls. It found its way into the Moslem world, the most spectacular use being, at one time, the bright red Moroccan sash. By the late Middle Ages, sprang was widespread throughout Eastern Europe. It has also been discovered among the Hindus of the Punjab, in Japan, in the Paracas caverns of Peru, and elsewhere. But in all this history, in the wide variety of objects made using the elastic quality of sprang material, I found no mention of hammocks. I had already produced my first sprang hammock, dwelling in a dreamworld of racial memory, contemplating the warp and the weft of civilization, when I revisited Ms. Brandford. "Hammock?" she said, "I figured it out myself when I wondered what might be done with this interesting technique. I was inspired by a Moroccan sash."

Well, it *looks* ethnic. Why not make up any story about it you want? In truth, the sprang hammock was developed by Joanne Segal Brandford at Cambridge, Massachusetts, in 1971 A.D. This chapter makes it known to the world for the first time: a historic event, and You Are There.

Overview

Although not as immediately spectacular as the Twin Oaks Hammock, the sprang hammock is, in many ways, much more interesting. On close examination, the weave itself is beautiful. It takes longer to make, with opportunities for experimentation. It is a more intricate technique, allowing the personal touches of the weaver. Because the sprang hammock uses string instead of rope, it produces a finer mesh, more yielding to the contours of the body. It is lighter, narrower, and generally less bulky than the Twin Oaks hammock. It tends to envelop the occupant like a cocoon. Some people prefer this, but others find it confining, and like to have a short spreader at one end.

This is what will happen: you will go to Sears or its equivalent and buy several balls of string and a few odds and ends. If you choose to dye the string, you will make it into skeins and boil it for some time. Then you will build a simple warping frame by arranging a series of pegs according to instructions. You will unravel the balls or skeins of string by wrapping them around the pegs and then tie up each skein to hold it in position. Next, you will build a simple loom out of dowels, screw-eyes and clothesline. You will transfer all the skeins onto the loom, arrange them carefully, untie them, and your warp will be ready with about two hundred strands of string, all in order, all roughly the same length. And now the interesting part: you will twist the strands together, a row at a time, following instructions blindly. For someone who has never done any weaving, the sensation is something like, "Look, Ma, I can tap-dance!" The work will proceed rapidly, developing its own rhythm as you reach top speed, becoming relaxing, even therapeutic. You will try bolder variations. Mistakes will be made, inevitably, but unless they are really spectacular, they will hardly be noticed in the final result. A single weft strand in the middle will complete the main body of the hammock. You will attach one end to a metal ring by making a web of dozens of single strands. At the other end, if you choose, you will make a simple spreader and connect it to the hammock with ten ropes, devised by a clever twisting technique. You will put the hammock up, lie in it, make adjustments in the interest of comfort, clean up a few last details, and exult.

Materials

Seine twine (cotton). Nine balls (250 feet). No. 36. About $1.50 per ball.

Clothesline. 30 feet. No. 6 or No. 7. Usually the least you can buy is a 100-foot hank at $2.60 and up.

Screw eyes. Twelve. 1½ inch. A box of 8 is 40¢. Exact size is not necessary.

Dowels. Three. 3 feet long by 1 inch diameter. 79¢ each at Sears.

Spreader stick. One Hardwood. ¾-inch to 1-inch thick, 42 inches long. A scrap of oak molding is ideal. (See Twin Oaks chapter, Section 3.)

Metal rings. Two. 2½-inch diameter. Zinc or cadmium coated is perfection. About 75¢ each at a large hardware store. If this item cannot be found, a loop of rope may be used instead.

Pegs, round or square. Five. Each about 1 foot long and 1 inch across (see Section 2).

3-foot flat sticks. Three. Called swords or shed-sticks to be used in weaving. Molding with one fairly sharp edge is perfect. One should be fairly sturdy, perhaps 2 inches wide or more, clam-shell type. The other two should be no more than 1-inch wide. To better understand what these are for, look ahead to Section 7.

Measuring tape.

One large-eyed needle.

Making the Hammock

Section 1: Dye the String. Optional.

This is a nuisance. I urge you to pass it up the first time you make this hammock and try it another time when you are feeling more confident and experimental. There's nothing wrong with a white hammock.

String is saturated with sizing, a sort of starch coating of the fibers. The dye will not take unless most of the sizing is removed. Wind the string into seven skeins by taking it off seven balls and wrapping it around two convenient projections about eighteen inches apart — or about as wide as Grandma made you hold your hands when she wound her yarn around YOU. Tie each skein loosely in four places. Boil the skeins of string for a good three hours, changing the water every thirty minutes. The sizing will turn the water a creamy color. A little Calgon water conditioner (any supermarket) will help remove the sizing. As for dyes: the usual dyes found in most supermarkets do not seem to hold up for our purpose. Better to buy Procion dye at a good crafts shop. Follow the instructions that come with it: they tell it better than I do. Your colors will come out as light pastels. Pink and blue are good colors. How about a pink hammock with a blue weft string across the middle and a white harness?

Section 2: Build a Warping Frame.

The warp is made up of all the vertical strands. It is important that all these strands be roughly the same length and all lined up in a row, none crossed over. This is accomplished by unwinding the balls of twine and wrapping them around a series of pegs, called a warping frame, and then, once the strands have been properly aligned and inspected, transferring them onto a loom. Think of this again as a fancy version of holding your hands a few feet apart while Grandma winds her ball of yarn around them.

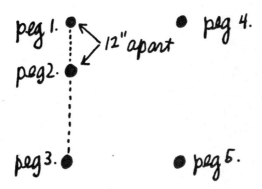

If you have a weaver friend, by all means borrow a warping frame. If not, follow directions carefully. Cut a one-inch by one-inch (more or less) stick into five ten- to twelve-inch pegs. You can use a dowel (round stick), but you may have trouble nailing round pegs firmly in place. In primitive countries, these pegs are often pounded into the ground, but you can secure them that well without all the work. Using a thick board or large old bureau drawer, or (my favorite) a door frame, nail the pegs so that:

1. A good five inches is clear for use.
2. Pegs 1 and 2 are about twelve inches apart.
3. Pegs 1, 2 and 3 are in a straight row.
4. Pegs 4 and 5 are placed in such a way that a

piece of string between fourteen and fifteen feet long can be wrapped around all the pegs once in a circuit (as in Figure 2). It does not matter whether the pegs are equidistant, or (with the exception of peg 1 and 2) what distance lies between them. As long as pegs 1, 2 and 3 are in a row, they can be on the left or right side, top or bottom of the frame. You could do without peg 5 altogether, but it would mean walking a few steps between peg 3 and peg 4 each time you wind around, losing momentary control of the pegs that are out of reach. Be sure the pegs are well secured and that all are straight. Crooked pegs will mean different lengths of strands in the warp. Smoothing off any sharp edges or corners with rough sandpaper is a good idea so you won't nick your hands when working fast. Wrap a fourteen- to fifteen-foot piece of string around the pegs to make sure it is the right length to run between pegs 1, 2, 3, 4, 5 and back, 4, 3, 2, 1.

Section 3: Wind the String Around the Warping Frame.

Find an end to the string inside the core of the ball. Put the ball in a large bowl at your feet, and let it bop around in there. Otherwise, the ball will tend to roll away and get tangled. Remove all cats from the room. If you have already wound the string into skeins for dyeing, return the skeins to their convenient projections, or some others, and unwind the string from there as you need it.

To make these instructions clear, assume the warping frame in Figure 2 is on the floor and you are standing at pegs 3 and 5, looking down upon it. Loop

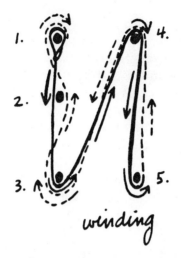

winding

the end of the string around peg 1 and tie it securely: a square knot or children's shoelace knot is fine. Be sure the loop is a little larger than the peg, or about as big as a half-dollar. Now wind the string around the pegs with steady, gentle tension, not strain, going to the *left* of peg 2, counterclockwise around peg 3, clockwise around peg 4, clockwise around peg 5, counterclockwise back around peg 4, clockwise back around peg 3, to the *right* of peg 2, clockwise around peg 1, to the left of peg 2 again, etc. Note the string is all the same, coming or going, around pegs 3 and 4, and it really makes no difference which way it goes around peg 5, but it alternates going to one side and then to the other of peg 2. The string is continuously crossing at a point midway between pegs 1 and 2, making an X, called by weavers a cross. It is important that *all* strings that you are wrapping around the pegs (the warp) alternate in succession between the two diagonals of the cross. Keep all the rows untangled. Every few rounds, nudge the strings so they are resting tightly against each other in order. When you come to the end of the ball of string, go back to where it last rounded peg 1 and tie it off there, again making a loop about the size of a half-dollar. Always tie on or off at peg 1. Frequently, you will find a knot or a defect in the middle of a ball of string. Cut it out, go back to peg 1 and tie it off. When you tie on again, be sure to preserve the alternating diagonals of the cross by going to the left of peg 2. Tie-on and tie-off loops can fool you by being out of line with the other strings. Continue until you have used a full ball of string. Tie it off and give the cross a final check to make sure the strings always alternate.

Section 4: Tie up the Warp Skeins.

This is to preserve the order of the strings so you can transfer them successfully to the loom: the cross is the essential element here. Using separate pieces of

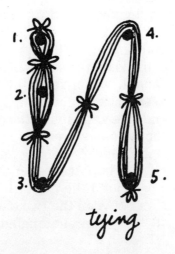

tying

string, each about a foot long, you are to tie tight bows, as on a shoelace. Don't be afraid to scrunch the strings together into a bunch.

At peg 1, run a string under *all* the loops along the far side of the peg and make a bow. In doing this, you will be going through all the tie-on and tie-off loops. This string will mark the exact location of peg 1 when you need it later. Next, tie up the cross. Put a string down through the peg 2 side of the cross around the bottom, up through the peg 1 side of the cross, and tie a tight bow on the top.

Caution:

1. In tying up the cross, do not put the string through any of the tie-on, tie-off loops; these are not part of the cross.

2. Each string coming off a tie-on, tie-off must be carefully checked in reference to its neighbors to see whether it goes to the left or the right of the peg 1 side of the string used to tie the cross.

3. Be careful not to overlook the bottom-most warp string (first tie-on) or the top warp string (final tie-off).

Between pegs 2 and 3, separate the warp strings into a bottom bunch and a top bunch. Run the tie string around the bottom, cross it between the bunches, bring the ends to the top of the top bunch and tie a tight bow. The warp strings will be scrunched together inside a sort of figure eight with a bow on top. Put your fingers where the tie string crossed over at the middle of the figure eight and trace along the warp strings until you can make the same two bunches between pegs 3 and 4 with another figure eight and a bow. Do the same between pegs 4 and 5. Finally, tie a string through *all* the loops going around peg 5, thus marking the location of peg 5.

Check everything over. Take the skein off the warping frame and set it aside, out of reach of children, cats, dogs and like hazards to the creative spirit. Repeat the process described in this and the previous section until you have used up seven two hundred fifty foot balls of string.

Section 5: Build a Loom.

Find a place to set the loom up, with good light and pleasant surroundings if possible. A closet door, the doorway to a spare room (you can squeeze your way around the loom once it is operational), a bay window, a porch, a clean attic, all offer possibilities. Take three three-foot long dowels (round sticks) about an inch in diameter. Put a screw-eye at each end of every dowel. This is easy if you hammer a nail in a little ways and then work it out to make a starting hole. Put a bit of soap on the screw thread and you can easily twist it in with your fingers. Build your loom according to Figure 4, using clothesline for ropes. Secure the loom by firmly embedding screw-eyes in the floor and in a beam or door frame overhead. Make sure the screw-eyes holding the top dowel are especially secure so they can hold a lot of weight. Tie the clothesline holding the top dowel securely before you load the loom. If you try to make adjustments to the top dowel once the spranging is underway, you may be surprised at how fast the rope can slip out of your hand, sending the whole loom and hammock to the floor in an obscene tangle. I

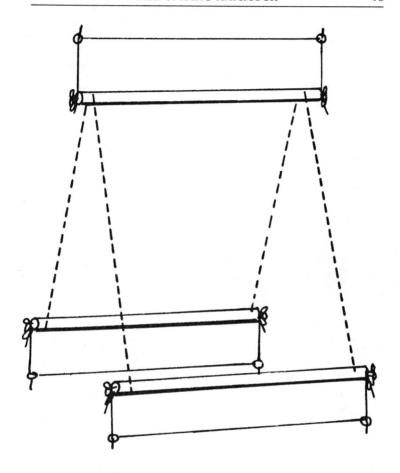

speak from experience. Tie one end of the rope on each of the bottom two dowels with a slip knot so they can be easily adjusted and let a few extra feet of string hang off the end. If, for some reason, you can not put screws into the floor, you can hold the loom in place by putting heavy cinder blocks on the ropes attached to the bottom dowel. This also allows you the delight of weaving outdoors, securing the top dowel to a tree-branch or an old swing-set. Incidentally, any holes you make in woodwork with this loom are easily filled with plastic wood or a ready-mixed spackle.

Section 6: Set up the Warp.

Now you will find out why you tied all those bows while the string was on the warping frame. You are to line up side by side all the skeins on the loom with all the bows facing the same way (except the ends that were at peg 1 and 5), without any twist in the skeins between the bows. This is a crucial step and easy to mess up, so take your time and make sure everything is done right.

Put the front bottom dowel through all the loops of one skein exactly where peg 1 was. This can be found from the string that was tied at peg 1 just before you took it off the warping frame. Check how that tie-string goes and make sure *all* the loops, including tie-on, tie-off loops, are included. Toss the rest of the skein over the top dowel. Do not untie any bows until later. Run your hand up the strings from what was peg 1 to the bow of the cross without allowing any twist in the skein. See if the cross's bow is on the left or the right side of your skein. Whichever side it is on, you will line up all the other bows the same way without twisting the skein more than a bit. By examining the cross's tie-string, put your fingers into the skein where peg 2 was located and slide your hand up to the next bow, the one that was between peg 2 and peg 3, unwinding any twist in the skein as you go. See that this next bow is on the same side as the last, put your fingers in the skein at the other side of the bow, slide up to the bow that was between pegs 3 and 4, undo any twist

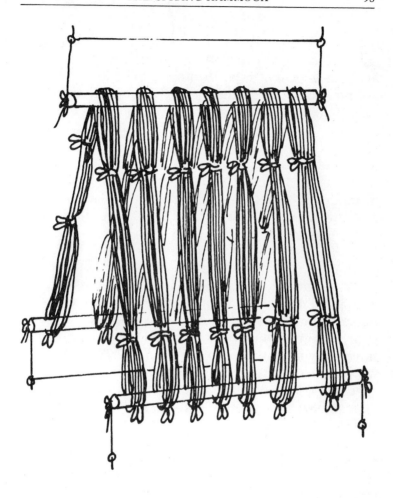

by getting the bow on the proper side, move on to the last bow, and, finally, insert the bottom rear dowel through the loops where peg 5 had been. By this method, you will have duplicated on the loom the arrangement of string that had been on the warping frame. Still do not untie any bows. Put the other six skeins on the loom in the same way, making sure that all the bows point in the same direction as the bows of the first skein. As a safety measure, run a five-foot length of rope through all the loops on the bottom front dowel and tie the ends of this safety rope together. Do the same for the loops on the bottom rear dowel. This is in case the loom should come apart and a few loops fall off the dowels. Also, tie a loose safety string around all the crosses, going through all the peg 1 sides, around, and back through all the peg 2 sides. This measure allows you to return easily to this point in the project in case of a weaving catastrophe.

Adjust the bottom front and rear dowels until there is some tension in all the skeins. Don't worry about slight variations in tension between skeins or individual loops: an inch of slack doesn't matter. Several inches of slack in one skein indicates that your warping frame pegs changed position at some time and you may have to rewind a few skeins on the warping frame. Take your widest, heaviest sword or shed-stick (the flat sturdy piece of wood, perhaps clamshell-type molding), and run it through the peg 2 side of all the crosses.

Now the exciting moment: untie all the bows. Look to see if you failed to put any of the loops on either the front or rear dowel. It may seem impossible, but I do it quite often. Tie any such stray loops onto the dowel with a short piece of string and don't worry about them until you are ready to take the hammock off the loom. Spread the strings out fairly evenly across about two feet of the loom, admiring your beautiful warp. If any string or strings seem too slack to you, you can tighten them a surprising amount by wetting them with a washcloth.

Section 7: Sprang.

With your widest, heaviest sword or shed-stick that is in the peg 2 position above the cross, push the cross and its safety string down against the bottom front dowel. You can push hard if you want, but it's best to work it into place with repeated short strokes. Then put a hand on each end of the sword with all the warp in between and "comb" the warp once by pushing the sword up the warp, squeezing it over the top dowel, running it down to the bottom rear dowel, and then returning it back up the warp, over the top dowel and back down until it is pushing the cross against the bottom front dowel again. Replace your widest sword with your narrowest. This is easy if you turn the wide sword on edge, opening the warp by separating the strings that are behind and the strings that are in front of the sword, then slide the narrower sword along the wider one until it is in place, and slip the wider sword out. Put the new sword in position by nudging it down against the crosses until it is parallel to the dowel. You will be spranging just above the sword, so you may want to adjust the loom to a comfortable height. The front and the rear sides of the warp need not be equal length until the end of spranging.

Basically, spranging means twisting with your fingers. Before you begin, read to the end of this section. I am right-handed; the instructions may be more comfortable for someone who is left-handed if they are reversed. Beginning at the right side of the warp, just above the sword, with the fingers of both hands, bring the farthest right front string counterclockwise around the farthest right rear string and back to the front again and then hold those strings in their twisted condition by feeding them onto the fingers of your right hand. You will have one twist in the small space between the sword and the fingers of your right hand and the opposite twist, less obvious, somewhere in the strings above. If you

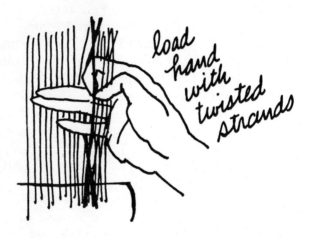

load hand with twisted strands

took your hand out and shook the strings a little, the twists would cancel each other out and you could try again. Continue working from right to left, twisting the front string around its rear equivalent, and preserving the twist by loading it onto the fingers of your right hand. If you give your right hand and the strings on it a little yank to the right before selecting the next two strings, the correct strings are more apt to become obvious to you. This is important because the strings frequently cross behind the sword and deceive you. When your right hand is loaded with twisted strings, replace it with the wide sword.

Slide the sword carefully through all the twisted strands—don't miss a single one. Also, be careful not to catch any other strings farther down the row on the end of the sword, because this may confuse things later. Continue twisting the strings, developing your own technique, transferring each load from

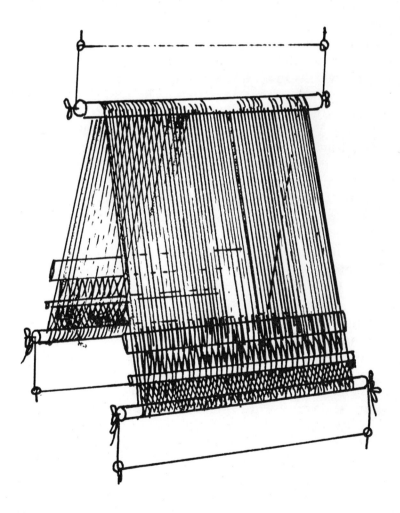

your right hand to the wide sword, until the row is completed and the wide sword passed through its entire length. If you have an extra string or two remaining in the back or front row at the far left side, twist them all together around the last available equivalent string. We will examine the left-over string problem in more detail later.

Put your hands on the ends of the wide sword and push it up the warp, over the top dowel and down against the bottom rear dowel. In this way, you will have an exact negative of the twist on the front of the loom appearing at the rear of the loom. Sometimes it is hard to move the dowel through the warp. You can apply quite a lot of pressure without hurting the hammock, but don't break the sword or you will have to do that row over. If a tangle of string is stubborn about going over the top dowel, work it over with your fingers, using them as a sort of comb. The rows on the far side of the loom are never as neat as the rows on the front, and any differences in the length of warp strings will end up there. The neater the better, of course, but don't worry about the far side; most irregularities will even out when the hammock is completed. Slide a light sword alongside the large sword on the far side and leave it there while you bring the large sword back up the warp, over the top and back to where it originally was. Remove the light sword already there in the warp above the bottom front dowel and scrunch the twist down toward that dowel with the large sword until it is parallel to it. Slide the light sword along the large sword, remove the large sword and you are ready to twist the next row. Let me summarize the sword-play:

1. You begin with a thin sword above the front dowel and work just above it.

2. You use the wide, heavy-duty sword to separate the twists you make and the negative that forms automatically above them.

3. You carry the negative twist over the top and to the far side of the loom with the wide sword.

4. On the far side, you remove the thin sword that is waiting, scrunch the row into place and put the thin sword back, this time in the same position as the wide sword.

5. You move the wide sword back over the top, remove the thin sword on the front side of the loom and use the wide sword to push the row you just made into position.

6. You insert a thin sword in the position of the wide sword and remove the wide sword.

In the next row, begin by twisting the farthest right front string around two rear strings. Do this for the first twist only, then proceed across the row as before, winding one front strand around one rear strand. By shifting the whole row over by one strand, you are creating a mesh. When you make the following row, begin by twisting the farthest right two front strings around one rear string and then continue as usual. Make about ten rows, alternating back and forth like this until you really have the hang of it. Always be careful to take the next front and rear strings in their proper order. The tightness of the mesh will be largely determined by how firmly you move each row into position with the wide sword. I prefer it fairly tight, with each diamond just less than an inch tall.

Now try some variations. Make a row with an extra twist, bringing the rear row to the front and the front to the rear. This changes the shape of the diamond. Try a row where you wind the first three front or rear strings around one on the other side, thus moving two places over. This creates a row where the strings cross without being twisted. If you make a mistake (usually by selecting the wrong rear string), cancel out your error by removing your right hand or the wide sword from between the twists and do it over. Everyone makes mistakes — the author, frequently, and even Joanne Brandford, occasionally — and these mistakes are often permanently incorporated into the hammock. Don't be discouraged; they can only be detected on close examination. I once suffered a total disaster. A child removed all the swords. When I recovered, I arbitrarily assigned every other string to the front or the rear row and went on from there. The result was a perfectly decent hammock which, in a small area, looked like a web by a laboratory spider under the influence of LSD. I strongly urge you to tie a safety rope to mark the locations of the swords whenever you leave the hammock unattended. Make your mistakes at either edge where they will not be noticed. If you discover that, somehow, you have four front strings and no rear strings remaining at the left side of a row, you can arbitrarily assign two of the front strings to the rear. Be sure that no edge string goes more than one row without being incorporated into a diamond. Never twist more than one string around another except at the edges. Continue spranging until both halves are as close together as you can make them, right up against the top dowel.

Section 8: Secure the Warp With a Weft Strand Across the Middle.

Without a weft strand holding the two halves apart, the twists will cancel each other out once the hammock is removed from the loom. The method I prefer is called Soumak. On the left edge of the last unspranged area between the two halves, tie the two farthest left front strings and the two farthest left rear strings all together tightly with the end of a nine-foot length of string. Put the other end of this string through a large-eyed needle. Working only with the *front* strands, move the needle across two strands to the right, around behind the two strands and back out to the front again, pulling all the string through until it is tight but not too tight. Now put the needle through the strands three strings to the right, including the two you just looped, around behind two strings to the left, through, across three strings to the right including two that have already been looped, back two, through to the front, across three to the right, through, back two to the left, and con-

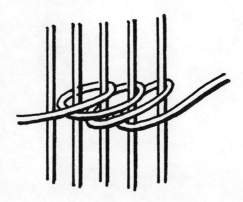

tinue across, advancing one strand with each loop. The loops will be diagonal to the warp strings. Position them against each other in a straight row across the hammock. The loops should be tight enough together so they rest against each other when the hammock is slack, but will open like an accordion when you pull on one side or the other. When you come to the far right edge, tie the front two and the rear two strings together in a bunch.

The main body of the hammock is complete. If any loops were left off the bottom dowels when you loaded the loom, redo the safety ropes to include them. It's not a bad idea to use the dowels themselves as an additional safety rope, untying the rope that runs through the screw-eyes in the floor and tying it again firmly against the dowel. Remove the hammock from the loom.

Section 9: About the Harness.

At this point, the hammock remains a pile of tangled string. It comes to life when a harness, or clew, is attached at each end. The type of harness affects the personality of the hammock. Joanne Brandford prefers to have a totally flexible hammock that is not artificially held open with a wooden spreader. I find the hammock simple and attractive like this, but, unfortunately, it tends to cramp my shoulders. This may simply be a matter of one's personal dimensions. The solution is to have a spreader at one end and not the other so you have it both ways. Spreaders at both ends would make the hammock tippy. The two spreader sections coming next are optional but recommended.

Section 10: Make the Spreader.

The spreader should be made of a hardwood, like oak, forty-two inches long, three quarters of an inch thick and an inch wide. It does not have to be as sturdy as the one used in the Twin Oaks hammock. With luck, you may be able to pick up a scrap of hardwood molding that will serve. Drill ten evenly spaced holes and round the edges as in Section 9 of the Twin Oaks chapter.

Section 11: Make and Attach the Harness.

You could duplicate the harness of the Twin Oaks hammock, using half as many ropes and attaching each of them, in turn, to an equal portion of end loops, being very careful not to overlook any end loops in the process. However, I don't find the contrast between string and clothesline pleasing.

A more attractive harness can be made by manufacturing your own ropes out of the regular string. Try this experiment a few times: take a few feet of string. Tie the ends together. Loop it over a doorknob or bureau drawer knob or some convenient projection. Stretch it out tight with the knot at your end. Put a pencil in the string where the knot is. Maintaining tension, wind the string up by twirling the pencil with your free hand as if it was the propeller of a rubber-band-powered airplane. Occasionally, relax the tension to see if the string kinks up. Give the pencil about twenty-five extra twirls after it begins kinking. Remove the pencil. Constantly maintaining tension, grab the middle of the twisted strings and double them over, touching the end to the loop around the doorknob. What was the middle is now the new end. Maintain tension so there are no kinks and the two twisted strings are lying right next to each other. You will feel the string wanting to unwind. Let it, slowly, by manipulating your fingers around the new end. Keep control as long as you can before it slips out of your hand. The two twisted strands will wrap tightly around each other, forming a flexible four-strand rope. Don't worry about it being unwound at the pencil end.

Once you have mastered this technique, make ten similar ropes, each one out of twenty-one to twenty-three feet of string. Give the pencil about fifty extra spins after the twisted string begins to kink up. Measure the ropes next to each other. You will use the ones with the longest twisted portions at the ends of the spreader and the shortest toward the middle. It is best to attach the spreader to the end of the hammock that has all the knots in it. Count all the loops that went around the bottom front dowel of the loom. Select the first tenth of the loops from one side. Examine them carefully to be sure you have all that tenth and no loops that belong in the next tenth have found their way into the bunch. Now use extreme caution: if you lose any loops it could cause a serious defect. Ease that tenth of the loops off the dowel and/or safety rope and onto one finger, then put the twisted (not pencil) end of one of the longer harness ropes through the loops. Open up that end of the harness rope by untwisting it a little, put the other end of the harness rope through it all the way and pull it tight until the hammock loops are all se-

curely tied in a little bunch. Do this for all the tenths.

Put the harness ropes through the corresponding holes in the spreader. It is all right to cut off the

knots used originally to make the ropes. Then put a metal ring on a nail or high bureau-drawer knob. Tie the harness ropes onto the ring so that:

1. When you push down on the spreader, it rests against the knot of loops from the main body of the hammock at all ten places.
2. The spreader is parallel to the floor.
3. There is tension in all ten ropes, none hanging slack.
4. The untwisted ends of the ropes and a bit more are surplus.

You will probably have to untie and retie a few ropes to get it right. Do not trim off extra rope at this point because you may have to make adjustments later.

Section 12: Make the Harness for the Other End.

This harness is a web of string, two strands for every three loops around what was the bottom rear dowel of the loom. Cut a shuttle (see Figure 4 in the chapter on the Twin Oaks hammock) out of a piece of shirt cardboard small enough to fit through your metal ring. Wind as much string around the shuttle as you can, making sure that it will also fit through the ring. Tie one end onto the ring, making a loop about an inch long so the knot itself can be hidden later. Leave a foot of surplus string after the knot so that adjustments can be made. Then run three and a half feet of string down to the hammock and pass the shuttle through the first three loops on one side, using all possible caution not to lose any of the loops

gather in groups of 3 loops

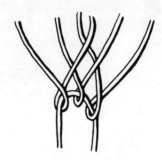

and to take the first three (and all the next groups of three) in their proper order. It is best to keep the loops on the dowel, if you can, so you can judge the correct length for each strand. Run a three-and-a-half foot strand back through the ring and, making all strands the same length, pass through the next three loops, back to the ring, etc., until your shuttle runs out. Tie it off at the ring, leaving a loop and plenty left over. Reload the shuttle, tie on again and repeat the process. At the other edge, it is possible that you may have to run your string through two or four loops. Making the harness strands roughly the same length keeps the edges firm and allows a gentle pocket toward the middle. If the center strands are too tight, they will form an uncomfortable ridge under the occupant. Put the hammock up (see the final chapter, on Installation) and remove all safety ropes. Back into it and loll around, trying both ends. If some areas seem too loose, if the edges hang down limply when the hammock is not in use, if some strings seem to press into you, adjust the lengths of the harness strands. You probably can make all necessary adjustments at the loose end and will not have to alter the ropes at the spreader. A few practice hours of lolling will automatically make most adjustments.

When you are sure you have it right, wrap the strands of the loose (not spreader) end near the ring with a ten-foot length of string, in the following way:

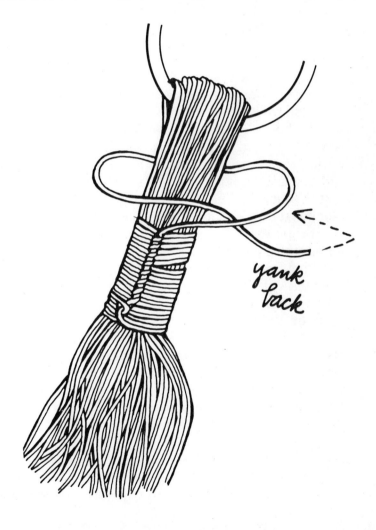

yank
back

Hang the ring on something handy. Trim off extra string after the knots. Put your hand around all the strings, just under the ring, and gather them into a tight bunch. Slide your hand firmly down the strands and tie the string around them tightly, three and a half inches below the ring, then wind the string clockwise once around the bunch above the tie-on loop, go past the knot of the tie-on loop, tuck the string through the loop you just made by winding around, and pull back, drawing the string tight.

Nudge the new loop right up against the tie-on loop and jockey the string around so that the lump where the string crosses over itself rests just above the knot. Wind the string around again, this time *counterclockwise* (so that the previous loop remains tight), tuck the string under itself, yank it tight, adjust the lump in line with the others, go back around clockwise, tucking the string under itself and yanking it tight every time, making each loop go round in an opposite direction to the last. Cover and hide all the knots and string-ends from the harness in this way and continue until you reach the ring and tie it off. This whole procedure will give you an attractive, tight finish to your harness, a solid white tube of string with a more or less straight ridge of lumps running up one side. Trim off unnecessary bits of string and safety ropes and you've DONE IT.

Section 13. Enjoy Yourself.

Settle back into your hammock with something cool and tasty. Relax. Let the feeling of accomplishment wash over you. You are skillful. You are competent. You have no more than one thumb on each hand.

Now start thinking about how to do it all better the next time. And why not try a four-color sprang hammock twice the size of the one you just made?

How To Install a Hammock

Homemade hammocks vary in size and ham-mock-lovers vary in the amount of tension or bow they prefer, so there is no easy formula about the height or distance at which a hammock should be installed. You have to find some help and stretch the hammock out where you think it should go. Remember, a hammock lies fairly flat when no one is in it, especially the Twin Oaks variety. Allow room for it to sag when occupied and room for it to swing, especially when it is to be used by children. Also, allow a foot or more at each end for tie-ropes, which will allow you to make adjustments. (Tie with the hammock hitch shown below.) Tie-ropes can extend

as far as necessary, but the height of the hooks climbs rapidly the farther out you go. The best hammock hooks come attached to heavy screws and are zinc or cadmium coated, costing under a dollar each. A heavy screw with an eye, on which an S-hook can be hung, works well, too.

Indoors

Indoors? Of course. Why think of hammocks exclusively as creatures of the outdoors? The hammock is furniture and the Mayan Indians have used them as beds, couches and chairs as far back as we know. Think of it: a couch you can fold up and put in the trunk of your car. Install your hammock on two hooks in your living room and when you don't need it, unhook it and put it completely out of the way against the other wall. Besides, some days it rains.

With the exception of many apartment buildings constructed in the last twenty-five years, almost all houses, including city houses, are built partially of wood. Usually there is a large post at each corner, and at the end of each supporting wall a 4″ by 6″ called a vertical supporting member. Behind each wall is a row of vertical wooden beams, studs, sixteen inches apart (legal requirement), measured from the center of each to the center of the next. These wooden studs were once 2″ by 4″, now they are generally 2″ by 3″ in name, and 1¾″ by 2⅝″ in fact, because the lumber business works in mysterious ways. Light laths or strapping of wood is put horizontally over these and plaster is spread over that, plasterboard in most houses built since the early 1950's. The object is to find a stud and put your hammock hook into it. Finding a stud is somewhat like dowsing for water with a divining rod. The standard procedure is to tap along the wall, listening for hollow sounds and more substantial thumps. If the thumps are sixteen inches apart, you're on target — in theory. There is a device called a stud-finder that costs about a dollar. This is simply a magnet that is supposed to respond when it passes over the nails attaching the laths to the studs. It never worked for me, but who am I to tell you how to find a stud? I've put up dozens of hammocks and it always looks like the back wall of the garage after the St. Valentine's Day Massacre before I am finished. I *think* I have found a stud, drill a hole, try again, thumping and tapping until the drill bites into something solid. A little ready-mixed spackle hides the damage. Don't be fooled by a lath that feels like a stud. Any doubt is probably correct. Sometimes, to be extra sure, I make a good-sized hole in the wall to see exactly what I am drilling into and replaster after the hook is in place.

I use a common electric drill with a quarter-inch drill bit. A note of caution: electric wires run behind walls. I once drilled into one and could easily have been fried. The quarter-inch drill bit was sheared off with a loud POP! Electric drills come with three prongs in the plug, the third prong being a ground to keep you from being zapped. If you have a two-hole wall socket, you will need an adapter to go from the three prongs on the drill's plug to the two-holed socket. These adapters have an insulated wire hanging off them with a copper hook on the end. There is a screw in the center of the plate that goes over the wall socket. This serves as a safety device as well as a handy way to attach the plate. Loosen the screw, fasten the copper hook under it, and you are protected. Don't use an extension cord unless it is three-pronged. Otherwise, you are taking a risk. I wear galoshes and squint when I drill, waiting for that POP!

Most smaller houses have wooden beams in the ceiling, especially easy to find in basement or attic rooms. Old buildings and lofts in cities have them, too. Sometimes I have luck with window and door frames, but don't trust the molding alone.

Brick or masonry is more complicated. Using a masonry bit on the drill, attach a board twenty-six inches long and *at least* an inch-and-a-half thick with three lag bolts. Back the board with epoxy glue for more security and put your hook into the board.

Many modern apartment buildings constructed in the last twenty-five years are almost hopeless. They have Sheetrock and metal slats in the walls and the lease is apt to forbid you to install heavy mirrors or paintings. One woman in New York installed a Yucatan hammock in such a wall and invited a friend over to try it out. At the apogee of an especially high swing, the hook tore free. Their feet smashed through the window of her apartment and they landed on their backs — fortunately inside the room. Outside was a drop of fifteen floors to the street.

One ray of hope: the windows of many modern buildings are framed out with brick, two bricks thick. A fortunate arrangement of two windows may work.

Another possibility might be to go into a concrete ceiling. For this, you need a special very slow-speed drill, about five hundred R.P.M., with a half-inch or larger bit. Use a lead anchor and put the hook right into it. This is really a job for a professional.

Outdoors

Shade is always a good idea. The usual metal hammock frame sold at suburban department stores is not big enough for many hammocks, especially the Yucatan one. You can sink posts in the ground, perhaps using a tree or the corner of a house at the other end. I wouldn't put in a wooden post smaller than a 4″ by 4″. Use a ten- or eleven-foot post and bury it three feet deep, filling the hole with crushed rock and dirt. Ideally, pour a cement base and coat the wood with something to prevent rot, such as creosote. Take this up with your friendly hardware store. Metal posts are less graceful but more durable. I wouldn't use less than two-inch pipe. Drill, or have drilled, holes at three different heights. Use a sturdy nut and bolt with an eye and hang an S-hook on the eye.

Trees are ideal, of course, because of their shade and natural charm. Any sturdy tree will serve. Even if you use a hammock hitch, rope will shift slightly as you swing, creaking and, in time, possibly damage the bark. It doesn't hurt a tree to use a hammock hook or an S-hook attached to a heavy screw with an eye. Hammer it part way in and wind it in the rest of the way by putting a screw-driver through the eye.

A hammock is dandy on camping trips if you are not troubled by mosquitoes. You don't have to fuss around with air mattresses or prepare your site. It's not a good idea to hammer things into trees you don't own. Use rope and bring plenty of it so you have more options. String a line over the hammock and drape it with a big sheet of plastic in bad weather. In good weather, lie under the stars. It's heavenly.